MARITAL
INTIMACY

MARITAL INTIMACY

A Traditional Jewish Approach

Avraham Peretz Friedman

JASON ARONSON INC.
Northvale, New Jersey
London

This book was set in 11 pt. Berkeley Oldstyle by Alpha Graphics of Pittsfield, New Hampshire and printed by Haddon Craftsmen in Scranton, Pennsylvania.

Library of Congress Cataloging-in-Publication Data

Friedman, Avraham Peretz
    Marital intimacy / by Avraham Peretz Friedman. — 1st Jason Aronson Inc. ed.
      p. cm
    Includes bibliographical references and index.
    ISBN 1-56821-461-8
    1. Sex—Religious aspects—Judaism. I. Title.
    BM720.S4F74   1996
    296.7'4—dc20   95-19974

Manufactured in the United States of America. Jason Aronson Inc. offers books and cassettes. For information and catalog write to Jason Aronson Inc., 230 Livingston Street, Northvale, New Jersey 07647.

To my beloved parents, Edward and Esia Friedman,
שיחיו, in grateful appreciation for their
guidance and love over the years

In Memoriam
R. Ernest Rubinstein, זצ"ל

Contents

Preface

This book presents a Torah approach to the exceedingly complex, multifaceted subject of marital intimacy.

Most Jewish books written today on the topic of human sexuality address themselves to the negative aspects of this powerful drive. A quick survey of the world around us will suffice to explain why that is so. The "free sex" society has resulted in divorce, disease, and a general feeling of discontent. Contemporary Torah literature has attempted to protect the Jewish marriage by emphasizing limitations of excesses.

However, it is not correct to completely reject all aspects of the sexual drive. In its own way, renunciation of the sexual element of life is no less contrary to the Torah's philosophy than is the world's obsessive preoccupation with sex. "Just as it is forbidden to allow that which is prohibited, so, too, it is forbidden to forbid that which is allowed" (Jerusalem Talmud, Tractate *Terumot*, end of chap. 5).

To emphasize the negative while ignoring the positive aspects of the Jewish outlook on sex results in a misrepresentation and, ultimately, a falsification of Torah ideology. A Torah-true view of sexuality can only be obtained by grasping the many disparate threads and weaving them together into one multi-colored tapestry. This book is an attempt to present such a balanced Torah perspective.

This book discusses a sensitive and delicate subject. In the pages that follow, we will encounter many statements of our Sages that laud the enjoyment of physical pleasure in general and of sexual pleasure within the marriage relationship in particular. In order that there be no misunderstanding, however, it must be stated clearly from the outset: Judaism does not countenance hedonism or self-indulgence. Pleasure is not an end in itself; rather, pleasure can be a powerful means of serving the Almighty and can enhance, and contribute to, proper observance of a Torah lifestyle. Although there is no inherent conflict between physical and spiritual (and, in fact, the two can contribute synergistically to a complete Torah lifestyle), overindulgence in and preoccupation with physical pleasure will necessarily divert one's thoughts and attention away from the spiritual. Indeed, one aspect of the greatness of the *mitzvot* regarding sexuality is that they enable us to successfully navigate between the two extremes, deriving the benefits of each, while avoiding the pitfalls.

> He should not withhold from himself all proper happiness and all proper pleasure, but he should be vigilant against the inclination to pursue physical pleasures without restraint and the danger in satisfying all his desires.
> (R. Avraham ben David ["Ravad"], *Baalei HaNefesh*)

Strict adherence to the *mitzvot* regarding sexuality brings the many benefits that this book describes. However, that is *not* the reason for observing the commandments. We need no justification other than this: *God commanded us to keep these* mitzvot. Any benefits that accrue to us are welcome extras, but they are not our reasons for performing *mitzvot*.

This book discusses the philosophy of these *mitzvot*; it does not discuss the *halakhot* pertaining to their observance. There are many excellent sources available on the halakhic aspects of these topics, and it is unnecessary to duplicate here what has already been eloquently discussed.

Regarding citations:

Page numbers for the *Zohar* are based on the Vilna pagination.

Unless otherwise noted, a source cited as

- a Talmudic source is to be found in the tractate indicated in the Babylonian Talmud.
- "Ramban" is to be found in the *Iggeret HaKodesh* attributed to the medieval commentator R. Moshe ben Nachman (the "Ramban," 1194–1270).
- "Ravad" is to be found in the chapter *Shaar HaKedushah* ("Gate of Holiness") of *Baalei HaNefesh* by the medieval commentator R. Avraham ben David (the "Ravad," c. 1120–c. 1197).
- "R. Yaakov Emden" is to be found in the section *Honhogot Lail Shabbat* ("Order of Shabbat Night") in the *Siddur* of R. Yaakov Emden.

Acknowledgments

Many people gave generously of their time and expertise to critique the manuscript. I gratefully acknowledge the invaluable contributions of

R. Yirmiyahu Abramov, שליט"א
R. Nachman Bulman, שליט"א
R. Yisrael Herczeg, שליט"א
Grand Rabbi Levi Yitzchak Horowitz, the Bostoner Rebbe, שליט"א
R. Meir Horowitz, שליט"א
R. Yehudah Lebovits, שליט"א
R. Aaron Lichtenstein, שליט"א
R. Ze'ev Haim Lifschitz, שליט"א
R. Mordechai Machlis, שליט"א
R. Jay Marcus, שליט"א
R. Dovid Miller, שליט"א

R. and Mrs. Yehudah Parnes, שליט"א
R. Ephraim Poliakoff, שליט"א
Mrs. Rivka Rapaport, שתחיה
R. Dovid Schapiro, שליט"א
R. Mordecai Tendler, שליט"א
R. Aaron Twersky, שליט"א

I assume all responsibility for any errors that might remain in the manuscript.

I thank the following for their editorial assistance: R. Kevin Aaronson, R. Mark Feder, R. Jonathan Mishkin.

R. Michael Unterberg, my *chavruta*, has never withheld his keen insight nor his sympathetic ear. The manuscript and its author have both benefitted greatly from his interest and friendship.

I gratefully acknowledge R. Zevulun Charlop and R. Chaim Bronstein for their encouragement during my years in the Rabbi Isaac Elchanan Theological Seminary.

Words cannot adequately express my overwhelming gratitude to Rav Yehudah Parnes, Rav Mordecai Tendler, and Rav Dovid Miller. Their guidance, wisdom, and personal examples serve as an inspiration and a constant source of encouragement.

While I was writing this book, I was privileged to be a member of the Caroline and Joseph Gruss Kollel in Jerusalem. Mr. and Mrs. Gruss, ע"ה, provided us (and countless others) with an incomparable opportunity to study Torah *b'nachat u'b'kavod*. Their legacy will live on forever through the Torah study they made possible.

My heartfelt thanks to my dear parents-in-law, Robert and Evelyn Harris, for their love and encouragement.

The truth be told, I wrote this book for my beautiful children, Elisha, Adina, Ayelet, and Akiva, שיחיו. I pray to the Almighty that my wonderful wife Marsha and I merit—in happiness and health—to see the fulfillment of the verse (*Tehillim* 128:6) "וראה בנים לבניך שלום על ישראל."

אחינו כל־בית־ישראל הנתונים בצרה ובשביה, העומדים בין בים ובין ביהשה, המקום ירחם עליהם ויוציאם מצרה לרוחה, ומאטלה לאורה, ומשעבוד לגאולה, השתא בעגלא ובצמן קריב, ונאמר אמן

1

The Need
for Contemporary
Presentations of
the Torah's Viewpoint
on Intimacy

Why is a book on the Torah's view of marital intimacy needed
today? After all, many generations of Torah-true Jews have
lived successful, fulfilling, authentic Jewish lives, apparently
without need for such books. What is different today? What
is it about our modern era that necessitates the production of
Jewish books on sexuality?

The answer is painfully obvious.

We find ourselves today in a world that is permeated by,
and preoccupied with, little other than sexuality and the seemingly limitless ways of creating and indulging sexual passion.
And, to make matters worse, even as the world wallows in

1

unbridled sexuality, it continues to instill the subliminal message that sex is evil and is linked inextricably with feelings of worthlessness, guilt, and shame.

This century's scientific and technological "advances" (among them radio, film, television, and other forms of electronic mass communication) have united the world to a degree unprecedented in human history. The power and influence of the various mass media is such that, today, it is impossible for any Jew or Jewish community anywhere in the world to remain insulated from the onslaught against fundamental Torah values. We are exposed daily to value systems and ideologies foreign and antagonistic to our own.

It is no wonder, then, that the Jewish community has unwittingly absorbed some of this confused ideology into its fundamental attitudes toward sexuality. Indeed, it is astounding that we have not adopted more.

It is natural to be influenced, in attitudes and conduct, by one's neighbors and associates, and behave according to the customs of one's fellow citizens. Therefore, a person needs always to associate with the righteous and frequent the company of the wise, in order to learn from their practices, and avoid the wicked who walk in darkness so as not to be corrupted by their example . . . So, too, if one lives in a country where the customs are wicked, and the inhabitants do not go in the right way, he should leave for a place where the people are righteous and follow the ways of good. If all the countries of which he has personal knowledge, or concerning which he hears reports, follow a course that is not right—as is the case in our times— . . . he should live by himself in seclusion. . . . And if the inhabitants are

> wicked sinners who will not let him stay in the country unless he mixes with them and adopts their evil practices, *let him withdraw to caves, thickets, or deserts and not accustom himself to the ways of sinners.* (Rambam, *Hilchot De'ot* 6:1)

The world has grown smaller with every additional scientific invention. In a very real sense, the desert the Rambam prescribed for people seeking to escape the detrimental influences of a corrupt society has ceased to exist. The assault on our beliefs continues unabated. Newspaper and magazine headlines, articles, ads, and editorials; billboards and bus-stop promotions; television commercials and sitcoms—all trumpet the same single-minded message. Against such a backdrop, the need for authentic Jewish presentations of human sexuality stands out in bold relief.

Why is there so much confusion as to what the authentic Torah view of sexuality is?

Once, authentic Torah views on, and instruction in marital intimacy were taught and transmitted in the most ideal, personal, and modest means possible: as they were meant to be taught, from parent to child. The nature of this subject, understandably, does not easily lend itself to public or mass discussion and instruction. Unfortunately, in our century, for many reasons, parental instruction in this area has dwindled, if not disappeared outright.

> There are young people who do not know how to observe the *mitzvah* of *Onah* . . . because, to our great sorrow and distress, in our time the inner bonds between father and son, and mother and daughter, have been sundered, and matters of intimacy and knowledge of

the private matters that transpire between husband and wife—which in previous generations were transmitted from father to son and from mother to daughter with love—are, in our generation, picked up and absorbed from the impure street and from other abominable sources, God should help us. . . . (*Midrachei Yosef*, brought in *Sefer Kedushah*, chap. 3, Letter 17)

In addition, many people with a rudimentary knowledge of some of the Torah's restrictions on sexuality jump to the erroneous conclusion that the Torah is against sexuality. They *choose* to remain ignorant of the Torah viewpoint, fearing that Torah knowledge will only serve to inhibit their enjoyment. How opposite from the truth.

We have an obligation to our children to teach them Torah values in all matters, not least of all this one, early on, before they are exposed to foreign, destructive ideas, in accordance with the principle that whatever comes in first makes the deepest impression. Bad attitudes learned because of our neglect will color and distort irreparably our children's attitudes to marital intimacy for a lifetime. One of the greatest gifts we can give our children is a clear-eyed, holy vision of marital intimacy, untainted by the corrupted, perverse notions of the non-Torah world.

One who studies Torah as a child, to what can he be likened?—to ink written on fresh paper. And one who studies Torah as an old man, to what can he be likened?—to ink written on smudged paper. (*Avot* 4:25)

To perform the *mitzvah* of educating one's children (which is a great *mitzvah*) requires great, wondrous wisdom and much Divine aid. A person should *not* wait to educate his children until they are grown; but, rather, from their birth—*while their souls are pure and untainted, and they have never tasted the taste of immorality*—their parents should begin to educate them in matters of Torah and they should introduce Heavenly matters into their hearts. . . . (Yeshaya A.Z. Margaliyot, *Da'at Hakedushah L'haRamban*, p. 14)

Part of the *mitzvah* of education [incumbent upon a parent] is that every father teach his bridegroom son the order and conduct of the wedding night, all clearly explained, while shame in such a case is foolish. Fathers cause their sons to face many obstacles when they neglect their duties and cover up in shame where elucidation is needed and demanded. In the *mitzvah* of *Tefillin*, doesn't the father stand by his son, guide him and educate him, and isn't he meticulous in his son's performance of all details of that *mitzvah? All the more so, then, in this mitzvah on which the entire holiness of the Jewish people and the future generations are dependent.* What should the son do in order not to sin if he does not know the proper and correct course of action? [These fathers] cause so much sorrow and dismay to their sons in their time of happiness, especially when they are brought to sin [because of ignorance of the Torah's laws]. Thus, one should strengthen and steel himself to teach his son wisdom and good sense, to make him understand and educate him. He should not conceal any detail from him. A woman should also teach her daughter, so she knows what will happen, because it is crucial for them (the son and daughter). (Yeshaya A.Z. Margaliyot, *Da'at Hakedushah L'haRamban*, p. 16) (Emphasis mine.)

Of course, before we can hope to properly educate our children, we must ourselves understand the Torah's unique perspective on human sexuality. This book is a modest attempt to reawaken interest in and discussion of the Torah's view of marital intimacy.

2

Judaism and the Enjoyment of Physical Pleasures

MITZVOT AND PLEASURE IN GENERAL

Any discussion of the Torah's attitude toward sexuality must be addressed within the larger framework of a consideration of the Torah's attitude toward the physical world and the enjoyment of its pleasures.

Many religious systems disdain the physical and preach that the triumph of the soul is achieved through the denial of the coarse, crass, animalistic body. Physical pleasure, these ascetic philosophies maintain, seduces a person away from spirituality. "Holiness," they claim, is attained by withdrawing from all physical pleasure.

The Torah does *not* subscribe to the notion of an irreconcilable struggle between the physical and the spiritual, and is, in fact, unequivocal in its rejection of this philosophy. On the contrary, the Torah maintains that, if used properly (as the Almighty intended and directed in His Torah), the physical becomes an invaluable and indispensable aid in the acquisition of spiritual greatness. This is accomplished in two ways:

PHYSICAL ACTIVITY
INFLUENCES SPIRITUAL DEVELOPMENT

A truth, in order to produce results, must be impressed upon the mind and heart repeatedly and emphatically. Merely to acknowledge the essential principles of righteousness and love is not sufficient to actually build up such a life . . . In addition thereto, symbolic words and actions are necessary in order that they may become indelibly stamped upon the soul, and thus preserved for yourself and for others. (S. R. Hirsch, quoted in *Tefillin*, page 5.)

The Torah uses the physical activity of *mitzvah* performance to engrave the significance of a *mitzvah* deep into the soul. Physical activity is much more effective at impressing an idea into the soul than intellectual contemplation alone could be. And, physical *pleasure* that results from the performance of a *mitzvah* serves as the means of achieving the deepest impression of all.

Almost every *mitzvah* consists of taking some "prop" of the physical world and using it in His service, in fulfillment of a Divine directive. Our job as Jews as envisioned by the Torah is to take the gifts of this world and elevate them to the heights of holiness. The *Shabbat*, for example, is sanctified over a cup of wine—words alone will not suffice. The *halakhah* prescribes *Oneg Shabbat* ("Joy in the *Shabbat*"), so we pass out delicacies—not *Chumashim*—to every person seated around a lavishly spread table. The very physical enjoyment of the chicken, wine, etc. is the fuel that propels us to heights of spiritual happiness and accomplishment. Similarly, almost every *mitzvah* consists of combining physical with spiritual, accomplishing, through this synergy, what each component alone never could.

> When Yitzchok Avinu decided it was time to bless his son, he requested of him, "Prepare tasty food such as I desire, and bring it to me so that I may eat and my soul shall bless you." (*Bereshit* 27:4)
>
> This request seems strange. If Yitzchok considered his son worthy of the blessing, why would he require a service as a prerequisite to gain the blessing? *The answer is that Yitzchok was preparing to make his blessing most heartfelt and earnest, by having his body participate through the eating of the savory food which his son brought.* (R. Avigdor Miller, *Rejoice O Youth*, para. 762)
>
> This is the system of all Mitzvos; to combine the spiritual with the physical; to elevate the body by means of its involvement in the service of Hashem. (R. Moshe Goldberger, *Techiyas HaMeisim*) (emphasis mine.)

After the Jewish nation received the Torah at Har Sinai, the Almighty commanded them, "Return to your tents" (*Dvarim* 5:27). R. Bunim of Pshis'cha explained that observance of the Torah in the purely spiritual environment of Har Sinai was incomplete and inadequate, and not at all what God wants. Torah lived in the context of our daily, physical lives— *that* is what God desires.

PHYSICAL PLEASURE INSPIRES APPRECIATION

In addition, the Torah lauds the enjoyment of physical pleasure as desirable, since each pleasure provides an opportunity to feel and express gratitude to the One who created
and provided this enjoyment.

The Torah begins from the premise that the Almighty
created the physical universe and presented it to the first
humans for their use and enjoyment. The myriad delights were
created for the purpose of bestowing pleasure on humanity.

Most people believe that the first commandment that the
Almighty gave Adam and Chava was a prohibition against
eating from the Tree of Knowledge. This commandment is
often understood as an expression of God's desire to forbid—
or, at least, restrict—the physical pleasure and enjoyment of
worldly delights allowed to humankind. The author of the
Meshech Chochmah, R. Meir Simcha of D'vinsk (the "Ohr
Somayach"), explains that the first commandment addressed
to the first humans was, in fact, a positive commandment:
"From every tree in the garden *you shall surely eat*" (*Bereshit*
2:16), followed only then by the qualifying restriction not to
eat from the one forbidden tree. The goodness and enjoyability
of the world and the creation of countless delights were not
mere frivolous, unnecessary auxiliaries, unrelated to the mission of humankind. The Almighty put Adam and Chava in
Gan Eden so that they could enjoy the pleasures and delights
that He had created. The prohibition of eating from the Tree
of Knowledge was a minor modification of the expansive
positive commandment to eat from all the trees in Gan Eden.
The Almighty allowed and hallowed much more than He forbade. The *Meshech Chochmah* concludes that the reason for
the failure of Adam and Chava to observe and abide by the

prohibition was their failure to appreciate the *mitzvah*-aspect of, or the Divine desire in, the directive of "you shall surely eat." They regarded it, instead, as optional, and neutral—something existing outside the sphere of *mitzvah*. The *Meshech Chochmah* maintains that had they truly appreciated and fulfilled this positive commandment to experience and enjoy all the delights of the Garden, they would not have succumbed to transgressing the negative prohibition, which resulted in their expulsion from the paradise of *Gan Eden*. Their failure to recognize the *mitzvah*-aspect of this enjoyment accounts for all of humanity's subsequent struggle, suffering, and turbulence. The Creator's creation of physical, worldly pleasure was not insignificant, frivolous, or incidental. As the *Meshech Chochmah* explains, physical pleasure is a vital, indispensable part of service of God, one that cannot be ignored or dismissed.

The obligatory aspect of this enjoyment of the *permitted* physical pleasures of the world is stressed in this statement of the Jerusalem Talmud:

> R. Chizkiyah the son of R. Cohen said in the name of Rav: On the Day of Judgment, a person will be required to give an accounting for all [permissible enjoyments] that his eyes beheld and he did not partake of. (Jerusalem Talmud, end of Tractate Kiddushin)
> *Korban HaEidah*: because he sinned against his soul in that he afflicted it for no reason [by withholding these delights].

This is where Judaism diverges fundamentally from other religious systems; this is what gives Judaism its unique essential character. Christianity turns a jaundiced eye on this world and its pleasures, and demands from its adherents a strict, complete denial of, and abstention from, this world and all it has to offer in return for a promise of reward in the next world. Any partaking of or involvement in things physical is condemned as weakness and compromise, a submission to the base, animal, evil desires contained within every sinful human soul. Christian philosophy pits physical against spiritual. Nothing, the Torah teaches, could be farther from the truth! Judaism teaches that only someone who has learned to experience and appreciate pleasure in this world, and has learned to express gratitude for these pleasures to "the One who spoke and created the world" will be capable of fully appreciating and praising the Almighty's greatness and benevolence in the Next World.

> Shmuel said: Whoever fasts (accepts upon himself and observes a voluntary personal fast) is called a sinner. Shmuel held, like the Tannaitic author of the following Braita: "R. Elazar HaKappar says: Why does the Torah state [regarding a *nazir*, one who has undertaken a vow to abstain from wine for a specific period of time]: 'And the Cohen will make atonement for him for that he sinned against the soul' (*Bamidbar* 6:11)? Against which soul did this *nazir* sin?—Rather, [he is called a sinner because] he has distressed himself [by abstaining] from wine. Now, how much more so: If this *nazir*, who distressed himself by abstaining from wine only, is called a sinner, then one who distresses himself by abstaining from all [nonforbidden] things, how much more so should he be considered a sinner!" (*Ta'anit* 11a)[1]

R. Leizer was concerned about observing the statement of Rav (quoted above) and was careful to save money

in order to taste of every fruit once a year. (Jerusalem
Talmud, end of Tractate *Kiddushin*)

    Korban HaEidah: he did so in order to bless "Shehe-
chianu" and to praise and thank God for creating good
creations to give people pleasure; blessed be He, the God
of thanksgivings.

R. Yehoshua ben Levi said: Only one who has learned to
sing in This World will merit to sing in the Next World.
(*Sanhedrin* 91b)

It is not in sorrow and sadness, not in self-castigation
and torture that Judaism reaches its highest level; its
holiest goal is serenity, gladness and joy.

    "Not in heaviness of heart and not in pain and not
in despondency," and not in frivolity either does the Jewish spirit find a lodgment. Where pure and thoughtful
joy dwells, there it dwells too. Frivolity flees before the
earnestness of the Jewish Law, and the Divine truth of
that Law drives away pain and mourning and teaches one
to live a serene, happy live on earth.

    The spirit of Judaism knows of no cleavage in hu-
man existence which assigns the spirit of man to God and
his body to Satan, by which the earth should belong to
hell and happiness should begin only in the celestial
beyond. "Prepare for Me here on earth a holy abode, so
that I may dwell with you already here on earth," says
the spirit of Judaism in the name of God. It takes the
whole being of man, both sensual and spiritual, into its
domain, so that even sensuous enjoyment becomes a holy
service of God when it is inspired with the spirit of modesty, temperance and holiness, and when man enjoys the
goods and gifts and attractions of the earth in a manner
so pure and acceptable to God and for such holy and

acceptable ends that he can raise his eyes cheerfully and
joyfully to God and does not need to flee from the
neighbourhood of His Sanctuary. To be able to abide in
the sphere of God even with his physical satisfaction and
enjoyments—this is the highest perfection of the mor-
ally-endowed man upon earth.

In no respect has Judaism been so much misrep-
resented as in this. Calumny has assailed it from opposite directions. For the sensual and frivolous it has been
too serious and spiritual, for the dreaming idealist earthly
and sensual. Actually it is nothing but Divine truth for
the whole man who is both spiritual and sensuous,
heavenly and earthly. (S. R. Hirsch, *Collected Writings*,
vol. 2, pp. 320–321)

The Torah, then, does not posit any inherent conflict between the physical and spiritual aspects of Creation.

The Torah's view of sexuality is a perfect illustration of
the general Torah attitude toward the physical world and its
pleasures: The Seer of Lublin (Rabbi Yaakov Yitzchak
Horowitz, 1745–1815) emphasized that a person must feel
and express gratitude to the Almighty when he experiences
sexual pleasure. Sexual pleasure, like all physical pleasure, the
Seer explained, is an opportunity to feel gratitude to God.

Although the Sages did not institute a formal blessing
(the classic Jewish method of praising and thanking
God) on the *mitzvah* [of intimacy] or the pleasure that
results,[2] nevertheless, a God-fearing person should
praise and thank the Almighty in whatever language he
understands for the pleasure he has experienced. Since,
in any event, he has had pleasure, he should offer gratitude to the Almighty, blessed be His name, for the plea-

sure he has experienced, so that he should not derive enjoyment from this world without giving blessing or praise; then the pleasure will belong rightfully to its owner and he will not have been guilty of trespassing and illegally using sacred things. (the Rebbe from Ziditchov, quoted in *Derech Pikudecha*)

And, as we shall see in chapter 6, the sexual relationship between husband and wife is the vehicle for achieving a very great spiritual goal: the pleasure that results propels the marital relationship to higher levels of solidity and vitality—beyond what intellectual interaction alone could accomplish.

CONTEMPORARY ATTITUDES TOWARDS PLEASURE

Fundamental to understanding the Torah's view of pleasure, however, is an appreciation of the dramatically different ways in which the Torah and prevalent Western society relate to the notion of pleasure.

Western society prizes pleasure. Much, if not most, of our time, energy, attention, imagination, resources, and money is directed to the pursuit of pleasure, in innumerable forms and varieties. Many times, of course, the acquisition or enjoyment of pleasure carries with it obligations and responsibilities. Often (though not always), these obligations are discharged and these responsibilities are fulfilled. What can you do? That is the price one must pay for many pleasures.

Contrast this to the Torah's view. The Torah also values pleasure, as we have seen—but with a significant difference. Duties and responsibilities are not the inevitable, unavoidable "cost" of pleasure. Rather, pleasure is a happy and not unwelcome by-product that accompanies and results from the proper observance and fulfillment of many of our God-given obligations. In such instances, pleasure introduces an additional duty to feel and express gratitude to the Giver of all pleasures.

Through a strange, insidious process of philosophical and cultural syncretism, even some Torah-observant Jews confuse the difference between these two lifestyles. They observe (with a fair amount of exasperation or righteous indignation) the attempt in Western society to obtain pleasure while trying mightily to shirk concomitant duties and responsibilities. This modern Jew "realizes" that every pleasure experienced brings with it a "cost" in terms of obligations, duties, etc.

The fallacy of this "syncretized" view is as obvious as its absorption into contemporary Jewish thought is dangerous. In this "modern" "Jewish" view, as in its non-Jewish source, pleasure—gratification of oneself—is of primary concern. Whereas Western men and women pursue pleasure while attempting heroically to dodge the responsibilities that accompany it, this modern Jew stoically, resignedly, and realistically accepts the obligations that the enjoyment of such pleasure entails. But, in both cases, *pleasure is primary, and obligations follow in its wake.*

That is *not* the Torah's view. Pleasure is *not* primary, and obligations are *not* the inevitable, unavoidable cost that one must pay or bear for its enjoyment. For the loyal, Torah-true Jew, duty and responsibility—to God—are primary; in fact, they are *everything*. If the successful, enthusiastic observance of God's commandments brings pleasure (a very common occurrence), then this is yet another opportunity to feel and express gratitude to Him. There is nothing wrong with pleasure that is obtained morally and ethically, but this must never be allowed to take center stage, as our duties and obligations to the Almighty are relegated to a secondary, inferior, or incidental position. Pleasure obtained through, *or as*, the performance of God's commandments is a nice extra—and one celebrated in countless statements by our Sages—but our gaze never falters or wanders from what, for a Jew, is the most important—indeed, the only—concern: fulfilling the will of the Almighty.

THE UNIQUE ROLE OF SEX
AMONG ALL OTHER PHYSICAL PLEASURES

Our analysis, while correct, is incomplete. There is another dimension. Sex is not just *one* example of physical pleasure. It is the ultimate, most extreme example because it is the most intense, volatile, pronounced drive.

Our analysis proceeded from a treatment of physical pleasure in general to sexual pleasure in particular. In fact, from the Torah's attitude to sex, the most extreme physical pleasure, we can extrapolate to all other, lesser pleasures because, *if a person can attain holiness in this realm, then certainly he can attain holiness through the rest of the world's delights.*

> The guarding of the *Brit*—i.e., sexual morality—is the paradigm for observance of the entire Torah. (*Zohar, Mikeitz* 197a)

The Torah recognizes the unique status of sex as the most extreme physical pleasure and acknowledges it in two ways:

(1) in the nature of the covenant of *Brit Milah* and (2) in the
rabbinic nomenclature for the sexually based positive *mitzvot*.
We will examine each in turn.

BRIT MILAH

It is not mere coincidence that the essential definition of
the Jew, *Brit Milah* (circumcision), involves the sexual organ.

> The *mitzvah* of *Brit Milah* proclaims the Jew's recogni-
> tion that God is not to be excluded from any human
> endeavor. (Yehudah HaLevi, *Kuzari*)

In his classic essay on the symbolism of *Brit Milah*, R.
Shimshon Rofoel Hirsch explains that our *mitzvah* of *Brit Milah*
consists of two *distinct*, equally vital, indispensable operations,
namely, *Milah* and *Priah*. *Milah* involves cutting the foreskin,
and *Priah* consists of freeing and exposing the organ (split-
ting the membrane and pulling it down to expose the corona).
Failure to perform *either* component renders the *Brit Milah*
invalid and incurs the penalty of "*Karet*" (spiritual excision
from the national destiny of the Jewish people). Both are ab-
solutely essential to the proper fulfillment of the Torah's requirement of *Brit Milah*.

But this was not always so, notes R. Hirsch. The original
commandment of *Brit Milah* addressed to our forefather
Avraham consisted of only one procedure, *Milah*. This was
the *Milah* observed by the Jewish nation until the generation
of Joshua.[3] Then, on the eve of their crossing over the Jordan
to take rightful possession of the Land of Israel, the Jewish
people were given another commandment:

At that time God said to Joshua, "Make for yourself sharp knives and circumcise again the Jewish people *the second time.*" (Joshua 5:2)

This [the verse in Joshua] refers to Priah . . . Just as the first part (*Milah*) is indispensable, so, too, the second part (*Priah*) is indispensable. (*Yevamot* 71b)

R. Hirsch explains the symbolism underlying each of the two components and explains why the two components were commanded in two different historical contexts:

Avraham Avinu stood alone against an entire world. His unique monotheism and the morality it inspired were in stark contrast to the immoral, depraved world around him. Because he was only an individual, Avraham's Godly morality expressed itself primarily in negative terms—that is, Avraham refrained from indulging in the immoral, uncontrolled sensuality and passion in which the rest of the world was sunk. Our forebears Avraham and Sarah were a lone family, and this distancing from immorality was the most profound form their protest could take.

When the Jewish nation stood ready to cross the Jordan River and inherit the Land of Israel, to the *mitzvah* and philosophy of *Milah* was added another dimension—that of *Priah*. The sexual morality practiced by the Jewish nation (from Avraham Avinu and his small family to the multitude of Jews who left Egypt), symbolized by the *Milah* (limitation, in both a physical and moral sense), was spectacularly successful. However, such morality as had been expressed until then would be woefully inadequate to govern and animate the life of an entire self-contained and self-sufficient Jewish nation living on its own land. A philosophy of sexual morality framed in negative terms, a lifestyle defined only in contradistinction to the conduct practiced by the other nations of the world, could not nurture or guide an active, dynamic nation and its multifaceted existence for very long. To the "refrain from evil" (see *Tehillim* 34:15) philosophy of old (symbolized by *Milah*) was added another dimension, the "actively perform good" (*Tehillim* 34:15) element (symbolized by *Priah*). The Jewish people would create a vibrant, thriving nation in *Eretz Yisrael* that would serve as a model of a national life lived in accordance with the Almighty's wishes for humankind.

After Joshua's generation, forevermore, the *mitzvah* of *Milah* has two components. Anyone who fails to perform *both* of these components has failed to perform the Torah's commandment of *Brit Milah*. One without the other is incomplete and inadequate, and *bears no resemblance to that which the Torah commands.*

The same goes for the philosophical counterparts that underlie *Brit Milah*. A philosophy that is characterized by withdrawing and refraining from sexuality (the "*Milah*" philosophy alone), a philosophy of sexual negation and asceticism, is insufficient and bears no resemblance to the total service the Almighty wants of us. Nor does He desire sexual license and lack of restraint—the philosophy of sexual behavior implied by "*Priah*" alone. Only in the harmony, the balance, obtained through the fusion of these two philosophical tuggings do we realize a true Jewish philosophy of sexual morality and conduct.

MITZVAT ONAH

The Rabbis also singled out sexual intimacy for special attention. Only two *mitzvot* are repeatedly referred to throughout the Talmud and rabbinic literature as "*mitzvah*," simply "*the* commandment." This nomenclature implies a certain centrality and preeminence among all the other *mitzvot*. What *mitzvot* did the Rabbis consider so fundamental and paradigmatic that they designated them, simply, "*mitzvah*"? Those *mitzvot* are "*pru urvu*" (procreation) and "*Onah*" (a husband's obligation to satisfy his wife's desire for marital intimacy)—the two sexually based positive *Mitzvot*. (See, for example, *Eruvin* 100b, *Pesachim* 72b, *Baba Batra* 10b, *Kallah* ch. 1.)

Why did the Almighty in His choice of *Brit Milah* and the Rabbis in their awarding of the universal title of "*mitzvah*" focus on sexuality? Why did they specifically choose *Brit Milah* and "*pru urvu*" and "*Onah*" if *all mitzvot* involve elevating the physical world? Why not choose some other activity?

No aspect of the physical world is subject to as much abuse as the sexual drive. That which Christianity writes off as incorrigible, incapable of rehabilitation, and antithetical to religious values and sensibilities is chosen as a symbol of the mission of the Jew to elevate the world.

The Torah is well aware of the seamy underside of the sexual drive. Still, it is not enough that a Jew *not* corrupt or abuse sex. The Torah requires that the Jew harness the sexual drive, that which is so easily corrupted, and use it for holiness. Sexuality is the most extreme representation of the physical world's delights, and *Brit Milah* and the *mitzvot* of procreation and *Onah* are the best symbols of the Jew's responsibility and mission to hallow these delights, while encouraging enjoyment of them.

One should know that sexual union is holy and pure when it is done as it should be, at the time it should be, and with the proper intent; and one should not think that there is any disgrace or ugliness, God forbid, in the proper union. (Ramban)

Just as hands, when writing a Sefer Torah in purity, are honorable and commendable, and when they steal or commit an indecent act are deplorable and ugly— so, too, were the sexual organs to Adam and his wife before and after they sinned. And just as each part of the body merits praise when it does good and condemnation and disgust when it does bad, so, too, was the case with Adam, with regard to the sexual organs. . . . All ugliness is the result of man's improper actions. (Ramban)

There is great spiritual elevation in sexual union when it is done as it should be. (Ramban)

This act is a [mere] coarsely physical act when it is devoid of sanctity; but if he sanctifies himself with modesty, then it is not considered physical. (Maharal, Netivot Olam, vol. 2, Netiv Hatziniyut, end of ch. 1)

This is its nature: . . . when it is good [when intimacy is performed in accordance with the Almighty's instruction], there is nothing as good; when it is bad [when intimacy is misused, performed in violation of His will], there is nothing as bad. . . . (R. Yaakov Emden)

Judaism is not content not to corrupt or abuse sex. The covenant of Milah and the mitzvot of pru urvu and Onah take that aspect of the physical world that is most susceptible to abuse and corruption and elevate it to a level where it is in consonance and complete harmony with the highest, most demanding standards of moral and ethical behavior.

We mentioned earlier that R. Bunim of Pshis'cha explained the Almighty's command of "Return to your tents" (Dvarim 5:27) as an expression of His desire that the Jewish people observe the Torah in all aspects of their daily lives, including the physical and mundane. In fact, the Talmud in Tractate *Avodah Zarah* (5a) also elaborates on this verse. On the Almighty's command "Return to your tents," the Talmud adds: "to the joy of *Onah*." This command, the Talmud explains, is the rescission of the prohibition against marital relations that had been imposed three days before the giving of the Torah. Perhaps we can suggest that the two interpretations are really one. When, as R. Bunim explained, the Almighty wished to express His desire that the Torah influence all aspects of the Jewish nation's daily lives, He could find no more appropriate example than marital intimacy.

Pru urvu and *Onah* are the paradigm *mitzvot* because they reflect the uniquely Jewish approach to sanctifying the physical world through *mitzvah*-observance. These *mitzvot* are the most dramatic examples of the phenomenon of elevating the physical world to the heights of the spiritual in that the element of the physical world that these *mitzvot* hallow is the one most susceptible to abuse and that is most often directed away from sanctity.

> The laws regulating sexual life and the partaking of food guide man already from his earliest stage of development. These Divine laws stand guard at the bridge which joins the material with the spiritual, man's organic-physical being with his Divine freedom. The eternal mystery of combining such opposites—and their continued integrity—is guarded by these precepts. Fulfilling these laws with thoughts and feelings of purity, freedom and holiness, ennobles those daily activities which often threaten to degenerate into vulgarity, indecency and spiritual-moral death. (S. R. Hirsch, *Collected Writings*, vol. 2, p. 330)

How different the Torah's view is from other religions! The Torah view instills neither guilt nor shame. The Jewish conscience is remarkably clear. The Jew is not plagued by paradox or contradiction. Against the backdrop of an approving, encouraging Torah, a Jew's intention in performing marital intimacy can, without guilt, shame, hypocrisy, or reservation, be completely "for the sake of Heaven."

> Wherever intimacy as a *mitzvah* is found—there the Shechina dwells. (*Zohar, Vayishlach* 176a)

> When a man unites with his wife in holiness—the *Shechinah* dwells among them. (Ramban, based on Tractate *Sotah* 17a)

> When the union takes place for the sake of heaven, then there is nothing holier or purer. (Ramban)

> Know, my children, that there is no holiness of all the types of holiness comparable to the holiness of marital intimacy if a person sanctifies himself in intercourse in accordance with the instructions of our Sages.[4] (Shloh, *Shaar HaOtiyot*, at the letter *kuf*)

The Torah describes the births of Kayin and Hevel (*Bereshit*, beginning of chap. 4) only *after* describing Adam and Chava's expulsion from Gan Eden (*Bereshit*, end of chap. 3) even though, in fact, Kayin and Hevel were born *before* the expulsion (see Rashi on *Bereshit* 4:1). Some commentaries explain that the Torah purposely switched the order in which it related these events in order that no one mistakenly conclude that sexual intimacy is sinful and that Adam and Chava were expelled because they had engaged in sexual intimacy.

"R. Akiva said: All the books of the Bible are holy; *Shir HaShirim* ('Song of Songs') is the holy of holies." (*Yadaim* 3:5).

Shir HaShirim, written by King Shlomo in his youth, is a metaphor for the intense longing and deep, passionate love that exists forever between the Almighty and the Jewish nation. When King Shlomo wished to describe this great love and devotion, he could find no more noble, pure metaphor than the love shared by a man and his betrothed. Similarly, in the Friday night hymn "*Lechah Dodi*," we pray that the Almighty take pleasure in the Jewish nation "as a groom delights in his bride."

3

The Spirit of
Contrariness and the
Ta'ama D'issura

THE SPIRIT OF CONTRARINESS

Within every person there exists an inclination to recoil from restriction or restraint and to desire that which is forbidden. This natural spirit of contrariness exists within every human soul, implanted there by the Creator, apparently for the purpose of providing every human being with the free will to choose between good and evil.

That such an innate contrariness, and consequent fascination with and desire for that which is forbidden exists as an integral component of the human psyche is attested to by numerous sources. Consider the following three examples:

1. King Shlomo acknowledges this innate tendency when he warns us that "stolen waters taste sweeter" (*Mishlei* 9:17).

2. The Jerusalem Talmud (*Yoma* 34a) states clearly that "One's inclination only desires that which is forbidden to it."

3. In *Kiddushin* 31a, the Sages discuss several types of people who are, generally, exempt from an obligation to perform positive *mitzvot*; a blind person is one of them.

> Said R. Yosef (a blind talmudic sage): At first, I was happy,[1] until I learned that "Greater is the one who is commanded to perform a certain *mitzvah* and performs that *mitzvah* than one who, though under no formal commandment or obligation, performs that same *mitzvah*." (*Kiddushin* 31a)

While R. Yosef's first, intuitive reaction makes sense, this final conclusion, apparently, does not. Surely, observance born solely and exclusively of love is superior to observance motivated by formal duty and obligation—so what is the meaning of this enigmatic principle?

Tosafot (*Avodah Zarah* 3a) provides the rationale for this seemingly illogical principle. One who performs a *mitzvah* without having been formally commanded to do so has done a tremendous thing, to be sure: he has performed a Godly *mitzvah*, an event of cosmic significance. However, one who performs a *mitzvah* because of a formal obligation has achieved *two* victories: he performed the *mitzvah*, *and*, in the process, triumphed over the natural reactionary recalcitrance that recoils from and rails against the first sign of restrictions and binding obligations imposed from without. In the first case, he performed the *mitzvah*, ultimately, because *he wanted to*; in the second case, he performed the *mitzvah* in the face of enormous resistance, against terrific opposition. This accomplishment of will is no less significant and praiseworthy than is the actual performance of the *mitzvah*.

DEVELOPMENT OF THE *TA'AMA D'ISSURA*

This inclination can remain within the soul for a lifetime, providing just enough resistance to prevent righteous conduct from becoming too easy or automatic, and thereby earning us reward in Eternity. In this state, it can be contained, controlled, and beaten—exactly what the Almighty wants. Or, something else can happen. This inclination can grow to terrifying proportions.

> R. Huna said: A minor convert is converted at the direction of the *Beit Din*.
> What is he coming to tell us? That it is an advantage for him, and one can act on another's behalf, in that person's absence, when the result of that action is to his advantage? We have learned this already [in a Tannaitic source]: "One may act for a person in his absence to his advantage, but one cannot act for a person in his absence to his disadvantage"!
> You might have thought that an idol worshiper [like a slave] prefers a life without restraint, because it is established for us [*Gittin* 13a] that a *slave* certainly prefers a dissolute life; therefore, he lets us know that this is said [only in the case] of a grown-up person who has already tasted the taste of the forbidden ("*ta'ama d'issura*"), but [in the case of] a minor, it is an advantage to him. (*Ketubot* 11a)

In the Talmudic passage quoted above, the Talmud discusses the procedure by which a non-Jewish child is converted to Judaism. The conversion of a non-Jewish adult is straightforward enough: the non-Jewish adult expresses his desire to become a Jew and, thereby, empowers the *Beit Din* to perform the necessary procedures to convert him. A baby, in contrast, does not possess the intelligence and maturity needed to make such a decision and appeal to the *Beit Din* to initiate proceedings on his behalf.

How, then, does the *Beit Din* convert a child? The Talmud explains that the *Beit Din* employs the principle of *"zachin l'adam shelo b'fanov"*—one can act on another's behalf, in that other person's absence, when the result of that action is purely and exclusively advantageous to him. In the case of a child (who, Rashi explains, is considered "not present" because he is not yet legally responsible), the *Beit Din* can convert him because his new Jewish status is purely to his advantage. This is so, the Talmud explains, because a child has not yet developed an appetite for the *ta'ama d'issura*, the taste of that which is forbidden. Once the non-Jewish child grows up and acquires this "appetite," the principle of *"zachin l'adam shelo b'fanov"* is no longer operative and the *Beit Din* would not be able to undertake conversion proceedings on his behalf.

What "taste" was the Talmud concerned about? What "appetite" transforms possession of a Jewish soul from a merit to a liability? Is it really not an advantage for a non-Jew to become Jewish—to acquire a Godly Jewish soul, with all the privileges and glories that accompany it—because he happens to have tasted, and liked, the flavor of pork, or lobster? Can an affinity for cheeseburgers negate the infinite grandeur of acquiring and possessing a Jewish soul? This taste preference seems small and insignificant compared to the acquisition of an eternity of greatness both in this world and the World to Come. *What a trivialization of the nobility and majesty of being Jewish!*

In fact, ham, lobster, and cheeseburgers have little, if anything, to do with the definition of "the appetite for that which is forbidden." The Talmud allows the conversion of a child, *not* because a child has yet to develop an affinity for *certain* things *which just happen to be forbidden*, but, rather, because a child has yet to cultivate a highly pronounced desire to indulge in any and all forbidden things *because they are forbidden*. The *ta'ama d'issura* is not an appetite for certain specific things (tastes, activities, and experiences) which, *incidentally*, happen to be forbidden. Instead, the *ta'ama d'issura* is an appetite—a gnawing, insatiable hunger—for anything, *as long as* it's forbidden; the activity's very forbiddenness attracts and seduces. A person who possesses (more accurately, is possessed by) a *ta'ama d'issura* craves that which is forbidden *because* it is forbidden. (See *Beit HaLevi Drashah #12* for a further treatment of this idea.) And *that* type of desire *is* sufficient to prevent the acquisition and proper care of a Jewish soul. That type of appetite *is* sufficient to prevent an eternity of greatness and spiritual grandeur because the Jewish soul stands in clear, direct opposition to this dark fascination. Possession of an appetite for such a "taste" *will* convert the acquisition of a Jewish soul from a merit to a liability.

The *ta'ama d'issura* is the most influential force that shapes and colors the sexual behavior of the non-Torah world, and accounts for many of its problems. This *ta'ama d'issura* comes in several tragic "flavors," among them extramarital affairs, incest, bestiality, and child molestation—and each flavor provides for the violation of some fundamental moral precept. Of course, each person has his or her own taste preference, but the common denominator is that the forbiddenness of each activity invests it, to the moral taste buds of someone who possesses this *ta'ama d'issura* (*and, today, who doesn't?*), with glamour, allure, fascination, excitement, sensuality, and sophistication. The most neglected of all flavors, the least glamourous of all (the "vanilla" of the bunch) is plain old *permitted* marital intimacy. The world invests intimacy with one's spouse with precious little glamour, allure, fascination, excitement, sensuality, or sophistication. Small wonder. Its very permittedness divests it of all appeal, and one of the only ways to invest it with any excitement or allure is to invest it with, or at least simulate within it, some of the elements of the forbidden.

An appetite for that which is forbidden can be developed in many realms and types of activities, but nowhere is this fascination for the forbidden manifest more than in the pursuit of sexuality.

THE PROHIBITION ERA—AN ILLUSTRATION

A recent historical incident provides a fascinating illustration of this thesis:

Once there was an era and a phenomenon called "Prohibition" in the United States. It was the intent of the architects of Prohibition to eliminate entirely the societal vice of drinking alcohol, and the dangers it inspired, in the United States. In fact, these well-meaning, albeit misguided, individuals were responsible for the unprecedented proliferation of these and a whole host of societal ills far worse than those they had originally sought to eliminate. How? How did their good intentions translate into such catastrophic results?

The process went something like this: many people just could not abide by this absolute ban on the consumption of alcohol. These people could not entirely suppress an occasional desire to consume alcohol. Of course, the very fact itself that there *was* a complete prohibition against alcohol went a long way towards heightening or creating that desire for the forbidden substance. Many formerly law-abiding citizens reasoned thus: alcohol does not seem particularly evil, and this absolute prohibition of alcohol seems extreme. The occasional harmless enjoyment of alcohol, they reasoned, does not warrant this kind of intolerance and heavy-handed intrusion, and the authority (government, police) that enforced this denial was dismissed as out-of-touch with reality. Many people "allowed" themselves the liberty of frequenting the numerous "speakeasies" (illegal establishments where alcohol, gambling, and far greater vices, among them prostitution and narcotics, could be obtained and indulged) that sprang up around the country, excusing their transgression of the law with commonsense arguments that the authority that would deny them occasional fulfillment of such harmless desire was ultimately unworthy of respect or obedience. From the well-meaning intentions of Prohibition's creators and supporters had come the greatest undermining and erosion of public obedience to the law. Slight initial antipathy to poor public policy blossomed into outright rebellion and contempt. Transgression of the short-sighted laws of Prohibition inspired a sense of lawlessness within formerly law-abiding people, instilled a willingness to stand in opposition to the law and its enforcers, and created a sense of resignation to the inevitability of such nonconformance to a legal system that was perceived to be incompatible with reality and human nature. The Prohibition Era inspired the creation of a new English word, *scofflaw*, used to describe a contemptuous law-breaker. This new public attitude was much worse than the transgression of any single, particular law could ever be. It is not at all surprising that, in such an atmosphere of lawlessness and contempt for the law, the infrastructure of organized crime was born and nurtured. Today, many decades after Prohibition's ridiculous prohibitions were repealed, a legacy of lawlessness and disregard for an archaic, unnatural legal system that has lost touch with the exigencies of real life remains.

The desire for sex is much more powerful, and fundamental to the human psyche, than the desire for alcohol. And yet, many religious or philosophical systems attempted to frustrate the expression of sexual desire. The historical transformation of sex from a natural, Divinely sanctioned activity (the Jewish view) to a forbidden activity (the pagan/Christian view) invested sex with all the dark, seductive charm that only that which is forbidden can possess. In the world at large, sex derives its capacity to attract, excite, and thrill from its very forbiddenness. As such, the enjoyment of sex is a function of the degree of its forbiddenness—that is, the more forbidden it is, the more enjoyable, desirable, and attractive.

The hedonistic modern man of today—his obsession with sex in the context of his relentless pursuit of all that is forbidden to him, his resignation to a career of religious lawlessness and consequent deep-seated guilt and shame—is nothing other than the natural, inevitable by-product and spiritual heir of philosophies that demanded ascetic denial and rejection.

In the realm of sexuality, the Torah acts in two ways. First, the Torah prevents the development of an appetite for the *ta'ama d'issura*. This achievement of the Torah is impressive enough, but the Torah does much more: the Torah even manages to enlist that inherent spirit of contrariness and turn it into a force for good.

TORAH CONTROLS ON DEVELOPMENT
OF A *TA'AMA D'ISSURA*

How does the Torah prevent the acquisition of a *ta'ama d'issura*? Let us consider several examples:

1. Perhaps the most dramatic illustration of the Torah's unique understanding of this powerful, volatile force is the law surrounding the *"Y'fat To'ar"* (*Dvarim* 21:10–14), the beautiful, exotic, foreign woman taken captive in battle. Astonishingly, the Torah permits this woman to her Jewish captor after a lengthy, involved ritual procedure in which she cuts her hair and nails, dons sackcloth, and mourns for her family for thirty days. This law is, at first glance, shocking. How can the Torah permit an alien woman to a Jewish man—a union severely, expressly forbidden during normal, peaceful times?

Some commentaries explain that the Torah recognizes the inevitability of such a union after wartime has stirred passions, and restraint and civilized behavior have been set aside. The Jewish victor is a man, after all, a man whose passions are aflame, and the Torah's call for moderation and restraint, so obediently adhered to under ordinary circumstances, is doomed to be ignored. Therefore, the Torah allowed this union in these unusual circumstances. These commentaries conclude that we see in this a compelling argument for observance of the Torah, in that the Torah does not legislate that which cannot be obeyed, and an indication that all its laws are compatible and in consonance with human nature. From the law of *Y'fat To'ar*, we see how readily "observable" are the laws that the Torah *did* legislate.

Other commentaries propose a different reason for this enigmatic law and, in the process, they provide us with a glimpse into the Torah's successful method for preventing the creation of a *ta'ama d'issura*.

This beautiful foreigner is captured on the field of battle when her Jewish victor's passions have been stirred and he is flushed with victory. The potential "*ta'ama d'issura*" appeal that she could possess—this forbidden woman—is incalculable. The Torah certainly does *not* wish such a union to be consummated, and it recognizes that the very fact of this alien woman's forbiddenness will invest her with the tremendous appeal that only that which is forbidden can possess. To forbid this woman at this time is to create and intensify a situation that can easily overwhelm the loyal Jew. Perhaps keen psychological insight and stealth may accomplish what brute force could not. "The Torah addressed itself to the *Yetzer Hara*," our Sages (*Kiddushin* 21a) tell us. The Torah permits her, not because it recognizes the inevitability of such a union, but, rather, because it wants to prevent such a union. It divests this woman of her *ta'ama d'issura*, her dark beauty and attraction. The Torah removes her forbiddenness, the source of her allure, and removes from her the gaudy glitter and tinsel with which the *Yetzer Hara* attracts us. Seeing her mourn her family neatly finishes the job of divesting her of any and all superimposed glamour and appeal. Shorn now of this "halo of *issur* [forbiddenness]", she presents a markedly different picture to her Jewish captor. He appraises her now in the light of clear-eyed, rational thinking: her forbiddenness is gone, and so, thirty days later, is her exoticness. Her hair and nails, the superficial trappings of beauty, are gone. He beholds her vulnerable mournful posture. Does he still want her? The Torah (*Dvarim* 21:14) concludes: ". . . if he doesn't want her, he must send her home." (See *Sanhedrin* 107a and *Sefer Chassidim* 378.)

Thus, the Torah neatly defuses a potentially messy con-
frontation with the shrewd, wily *Yetzer Hara.*

2. In the times of the *Beit HaMikdash*, there was a man
(the *"Ish Iti"*) appointed every year to lead a goat on the *fast
day* of Yom Kippur on the long journey to Azazel (see *VaYikra*
16). Consider the following passage from the Jerusalem Talmud (*Yoma* 34a) that describes his journey:

> Mishnah (*Yoma* 6:4,5): There were ten booths (way sta-
> tions) along his route . . . At every booth, they would
> tell him, "Here is food and water . . ."

> Gemara: "At every booth, they would tell him, 'Here is
> food and water'": They said this in order to restore his
> strength [even though it never happened once that an *Ish
> Iti* needed to eat the food (*Korban HaEidah* commentary,
> based on Babylonian Talmud, *Yoma* 67a]. Why [how did
> this practice restore his strength if, in fact, no *Ish Iti* ever
> ate the prepared food]? Because a person's evil inclina-
> tion only desires that which is forbidden to it. . . .

> 3.

> Yalta said to her husband R. Nachman: For all that the
> Torah forbade, it permitted something comparable: It
> forbade consuming animal blood, but it permitted the
> liver; . . . it forbade marrying a brother's ex-wife, but
> it permitted the leviritical marriage; it forbade a non-
> Jewish woman, but it permitted the *Y'faht To'ar.* I want
> to taste the taste of meat and milk. (*Chullin* 109b)

Yalta, R. Nachman's wife, introduces her unusual request
to her husband with the observation that "all that the Torah
forbade, it permitted . . . ," *as if this were not just a coincidence,*

but rather, a principle. It is, and R. Nachman is able to provide his wife with an equivalent culinary experience.

That such a counterpart exists, she is certain; it *must* exist. The comforting, consoling knowledge that there is some permitted outlet for the expression or satisfaction of every desire and instinct accounts for the natural self-control, moderation, and restraint that characterizes the Torah-true Jewish character.

The Torah's lesson is clear: If you forbid, you create the conditions necessary for fascination, obsession, and abuse to exist. If you allow, *even while circumscribing its use and enjoyment,* you avoid investing the activity or object with the dark exciting enchantment that the forbidden partakes of.

The Torah, philosophically and historically, has always actively and enthusiastically encouraged both marriage and sexual intimacy within the marital relationship. Indeed, the Hebrew word for marriage, *Kiddushin,* means "sanctification" and reflects this very Jewish attitude towards marriage. *Not* to be married, and thus *not* to be sexually intimate with a spouse, earn the Torah's sharp censure.

> R. Elazar said: Any man who is not married is not a man, as it is said, "Male and female He created them . . . , and He called them [together] 'Adam' (hu/man)" (*Bereshit* 5:2). (*Yevamot* 63a)

> R. Chiya bar Gomda said: . . .he is not a complete man, as it is said, "And He blessed them, and He called them 'Adam'" (Bereshit 5:2)—both of them together are called' Adam'. (*Bereshit Rabbah* 17:2)

> R. Tanchum said in the name of R. Choniloi: Any man who does not have a wife dwells without *happiness,* without *blessing,* without *goodness.* . . . In Eretz Yisrael

they said: [also] without *Torah*, without *protection*. . . .
Rabbah bar Ulla said: [also] without *peace*. . . . R. Yaakov
taught: [also] without a *helper*, without *atonement*. . . .
R. Yehoshua of Sachnin said in the name of R. Levi: also
without *life*. . . . (*Yevamot* 62b and *Bereshit Rabbah* 17:2)

"Any Cohen who is not married is forbidden to perform
the Divine service, as it is written: 'And he [the High
Priest] shall atone for himself and his home ['home'
refers to his wife (*Yoma* 13a)]' (*Vayikra* 16:17). R. Yitzchak said: Because the Divine Presence does not rest on
one who is not married, and the Cohanim need more
than anyone else in the nation to have the Divine Presence rest upon them. . . ."[2] (*Zohar*, *Nasso* 145b)

Through its encouragement of marriage and marital
intimacy, the Torah prevents the development of a *ta'ama
d'issura*. Within a pure Torah lifestyle, it is extraordinarily
difficult to acquire such an appetite.

Christianity's grudging compromise to the inevitable in-
ability and failure of the masses to realize the supposedly "high
ideal" of celibacy was permission to marry because, after all,
"it's better to marry than burn in hell." This provided the
perfect milieu, and historical mindset, within which to cultivate the *ta'ama d'issura*, just as the historic prohibition of
alcohol inspired severe abuse of alcohol. Even though, in the
end, marriage *was* allowed, the stigma attached to intimacy
through the knowledge of Christianity's philosophical disap-
proval left the most powerful, enduring impression on the
Christian consciousness.

Church censors demanded that the statement of R.
Elazar quoted above be changed in printings of the

Talmud to read "Any *Jew* who is not married is not a Jew. . . ." This Talmudic sentiment stood in bold opposition to the celibacy they prized so highly. (R. Adin Steinsaltz, *The Essential Talmud*, p. 85)

Contrast the statement of the *Zohar* quoted above with the Church requirement that a priest, monk, nun, etc. be unmarried and celibate.

THE SPIRIT OF CONTRARINESS IN THE SERVICE OF TORAH

If that were the extent of the Torah's remarkable triumph over the *ta'ama d'issura*, we should have ample cause to marvel.

In fact, the Torah does much more. The Torah deftly enlists even the natural contrariness that we described above in the service of moral, Godly living.

How? Every month, a woman becomes a *niddah* for at least twelve (eleven, in some Sephardic communities) days. During that time, any and all physical contact between husband and wife is forbidden, and transgression of these laws can carry some severe penalties. In addition to all the other wonderful things going on during those twelve days to ensure the happy reunion of the couple and the rejuvenation and revitalization of the marriage bond (some of which I described in my first book, *Table for Two* [Targum Press]), there is another phenomenon at work. For those twelve days the woman is forbidden to her husband. If, in every human soul, there is some resistance against restriction and concomitant desire for that which is forbidden, then the Torah injects just enough restriction into the marriage relationship to enhance the attraction of husband to wife, and wife to husband.[3] The reunion of husband and wife is incomparably more satisfying thanks to this "*ta'ama d'issura* turned *ta'ama d'heteira* [appetite for that which is permitted]".

The non-Jewish world finds the creation and satisfaction of the *ta'ama d'issura outside* marriage, in violent opposition to it. The Jewish nation finds the satisfaction of this "taste" *inside* marriage, in cooperation and harmony with marriage. In the Torah's system, even the natural reflexive spirit of contrariness becomes a means of enhancing and rejuvenating marriage.

The Torah's attitude towards sexuality, far from inspiring feelings of worthlessness, shame, lawlessness, immorality, and inadequacy, produces a very different set of emotions: contentment, pride, confidence, loyalty, morality.

The Jewish attitude toward sexuality is remarkably free of guilt or shame. In a Torah philosophy, sex should inspire about as much guilt or shame as the eating of *matzah* should— that is, none. Both are *mitzvot* of the Almighty, both to be performed with the same joy, gratitude, and loyalty toward the Almighty.

Upon hearing the Torah's laws surrounding sexuality, don't mistake moderation for guilt, nor modesty for shame. The Torah requires moderation and modesty in one's sexual behavior, but never guilt or shame. Observance of the Torah's laws and spirit promotes psychological health in a Jew who can be confident and proud of the Almighty's unequivocal approval of *all* facets of his life.

> When marital intimacy is performed "for the sake of Heaven,"[4] no act is more holy than it. . . . The fact that

the marital act requires privacy and modesty is due [*not* to any intrinsic degradation or inherent baseness, but, rather] to this lofty incomparable holiness. (R. Yaakov Emden)

4

A *Tahvlin*

THE RELATIONSHIP BETWEEN TORAH AND THE *YETZER HARA*

בראתי יצר הרע, ובראתי לו תורה תבלין
(*kiddushin* 30B)

This quote, which the Talmud attributes homiletically to the Almighty, is usually translated in the following way: "I created the *yetzer hara*, and I created the Torah as its antidote." This is a reasonable rendering into English. However, it is not completely accurate, for it fails to capture an important nuance. "*Tavlin*" does *not* mean "antidote"—that is, not unless you use ketchup, relish, or mustard to serve *as an antidote* to your hamburger, hot dog, or steak. More accurately, "*tavlin*" means spice, or condiment, *and a spice is used to enhance and complement that which it accompanies, as opposed to an antidote which counters, opposes, or negates.*

So let's look at that quote again: "I created the *yetzer hara*, and I created the Torah as its spice."

Ideally, the Torah is not intended to oppose or negate the *yetzer hara*. Rather, it is meant to "enhance" it—that is, to

43

channel the tremendous reservoir of energy contained in the
yetzer hara into the performance of *mitzvot* and the attainment
of holiness.

Torah is the "*tavlin*," the spice, to the *yetzer hara*. It does
not *nullify* the influence of the *yetzer hara*. Rather, the relationship of the Torah to the *yetzer hara* is that of a spice to a
sharp, strong, pungent food—that is, the spice enhances the
flavor of the otherwise distasteful or inedible food and creates a pleasing overall taste. Spice and food work together to
create an overall taste that neither alone could produce. (See
Iyun Yaakov to *Ein Yaakov, Kiddushin* 30). But note: a spice
functions as an aid, a modifier, an accessory to the main, cen-
tral taste which is the food—not the reverse. A spice serves
to highlight and enhance the food it accompanies. Consider again the analogy given in Tractate *Kiddushin*; this
relationship is significant—and surprising. What, according to the Talmud, is the main food and what is its spice, its
accompaniment?[1]

In light of this new interpretation of the quote in Tractate
Kiddushin, it is now necessary to reevaluate what is meant by
the term "*yetzer hara*." The approximate, or intuitive, understanding of this term, which has sufficed until now, is clearly
inadequate to explain this provocative statement.

A DEFINITION OF THE *YETZER HARA*

Usually, "*yetzer hara*" is understood to be the "evil inclination"—that is, that incorrigible instinct within a person that
attempts to seduce him and lead him to perform that which
is evil or forbidden. Support for this definition can be found
in talmudic statements that appear unequivocally condemn-

ing of the *yetzer hara*, one of which is, "Hard is the *yetzer hara*, for even its Creator called it 'evil,' as it is said, 'The *yetzer* of man's heart is evil from his youth' (*Bereshit* 8:21)" (*Kiddushin* 30b).

This description of the *yetzer hara* is, however, problematic in that, even as it illuminates many statements, it will render an equal number of talmudic statements incomprehensible. For example, consider the following statements regarding the *yetzer hara*:

> "The Almighty saw everything He had made; and it was *very* good . . ." (*Bereshit* 1:31): "It was good"—this refers to the *Yetzer Tov*. "It was *very* good"—this refers to the *Yetzer Hara*. Is the *Yetzer Hara*, then, "very good?" Astonishing! However, this teaches you that were it not for the *Yetzer Hara*, no person would build a home, marry, have children, or engage in business. (*Bereshit Rabbah* 9:7)

> Our forefather Avraham made his *Yetzer Hara* good. (Jerusalem Talmud, *Brachot* 9:5)

> "And you (sing.) shall love God with all your heart [lit., hearts] . . ." (*Dvarim* 6:5). "With all your heart [lit., hearts]": with both your inclinations—that is, your *Yetzer Tov* and *Yetzer Hara*. (*Brachot* 9:5)

For these and many other similar statements scattered throughout the Talmud and rabbinic literature, the approximate, intuitive understanding of the *yetzer hara*—the one which is usually proffered and accepted without any real serious critical evaluation—is sorely inadequate and clearly unable to reflect or capture this ability of the *yetzer hara* to change its fundamental character in different circumstances. An accurate description of the *yetzer hara* must incorporate and reflect this flexibility.

A better, more accurate, definition of what the *yetzer hara* is, one that accommodates the numerous, seemingly irreconcilable descriptions of what the *yetzer hara* is and does and that accounts for the different "personalities" the *yetzer hara* demonstrates at different times and under different conditions, is offered by R. Avraham, the son of the Rambam, when he writes:

> The yetzer tov is the intellect; the yetzer hara is bodily desire and other such desires. (R. Avraham ben HaRambam, *Discourse on Aggadah*)

Similarly, R. Mendel Weinbach writes:

> [T]he yetzer ha-ra [is] one's evil inclination, one's desires, one's animalistic drives and instincts that are undisciplined by his intellect and his inclination to do the will of God (*yetzer ha-tov*). (R. Mendel Weinbach, *Teshuvah in Our Times, Living with Torah*, Vol. 2)

The *yetzer hara*, then, is associated with a person's repertoire of drives and the free, unfettered, unrestrained expression of those drives; the *yetzer tov*, with the intellectual faculties and the control one exercises over those drives. The *yetzer hara* is the source of the drive for satisfaction of physical desires, among them the desire for self-preservation, food, shelter, and sexual gratification. And, as the spice to the *yetzer hara*, the Torah shapes and directs this reservoir of raw, undisciplined, impulsive, instinctive desire. The *yetzer hara* can be a powerful, incomparable source of energy to be used in the service of God.

> "'And you (sing.) shall love God with all your heart (lit., hearts) . . .": with both your *Yetzers*" (*Brachot* 9:5): the *Yetzer Hara* consists of those things which the body enjoys and craves, and one must accept upon himself to use them in the service of his Creator. (Rabeinu Yonah, *Shaarei Avodah*)

> . . . [T]he good yetzer usually appears in the Talmudic and other Rabbinic sources as "*yetzer tov*," meaning absolutely [intrinsically] good, whereas the evil yetzer is "*yetzer hara*," which may be translated as yetzer of evil [intention]—i.e., with a tendency for evil,[2] rather than "*yetzer ra*," which would mean absolutely evil. (R. Naphtali Wiesner, *In His Own Image*, pp. 98–99)

> God (who is called "Righteous and Just" (*Dvarim* 32:4)) only created the human "in His image" in order to be righteous and just like Himself.
>
> Perhaps you will say: Why did He create the *Yetzer Hara* (regarding which it is written: "The *Yetzer* of man's heart is evil from his youth" (*Bereshit* 8:21))? You say that it is evil; who can make it good?
>
> Said God: *You make it evil!* . . .
>
> Perhaps you will say: No man can guard himself [from being corrupted]!
>
> Said God: *You made it evil!* . . .There are many things in the world that are harder and more bitter than the *Yetzer Hara*, and you sweeten them . . . If you can sweeten for your needs those bitter things I created, how much more so [can you sweeten] the *Yetzer Hara* which is delivered into your hands! (Midrash *Tanchuma, Bereshit* 7)

All the acts of Creation [including the *yetzer hara*] are good: for the *yetzer hara* also aids the righteous, and the essence of their service [of God] is through it, as is known. (Vilna Gaon, *Be'urei Aggadot* on *Brachot* 61b)
    The essence of service of God is through the yetzer hara. (Vilna Gaon, *Even Shleimah* 4:2)

"I shall thank God with *all* my heart" (*Tehillim* 9:2): with the yetzer tov and with the *yetzer hara*. (Midrash *Tehillim* 9:5)

The various physical desires are necessary for the service of God and for the maintenance of the body, and one must subdue, not destroy, them . . . one must rule over the physical desires and use them for those things that are necessary and subdue [them and refrain from] the excesses. (Vilna Gaon, *Mishlei* 16:32)

The drives of man are varied, but the ways of responding to them can be put into two categories: the impulsive and the deliberate reaction. By impulsive we mean a reaction which gives the drives, innate or acquired, full autonomy, without interference by the intellect, while the deliberate reaction is one in which the alternatives are examined and evaluated, including consideration of their long-term effects, before a decision is made.
    Perhaps we are justified in identifying the evil inclination with the impulsive and the good inclination with the deliberate mode of reacting. (Leo Levi, *Torah and Science*, p. 99)

5

The Torah's Encouragement of Procreation

In the preceding chapter, we presented a deeper, more refined description of the *yetzer hara*. Supported by compelling Torah sources, we portrayed the *yetzer hara* as the repertoire of instinctive physical drives. We discussed briefly the Almighty's instruction to use the Torah as a "spice" for the *yetzer hara* in order to make its acquisitions and accomplishments more agreeable and palatable.

We also noted that this repertoire of drives contains, along with the desires for food, shelter, and protection, the desire for sexual gratification. How does the Torah shape and direct this desire to Godly ends?

Sexual activity, of course, allows for the fulfillment of the Torah's first positive *mitzvah*, "*pru urvu*," the commandment to "be fruitful and multiply," and this *mitzvah* is particularly beloved to the Almighty.

God did not create the earth a wasteland; He formed it
to be inhabited. . . . (Isaiah 45:18)

The world was only created for procreation. (Jerusalem
Talmud, *Gittin* 4:5)

R. Avin said: The Holy One, blessed be He, cherishes
[the *mitzvah* of] procreation more than the Holy Temple.
How do we know this? [For it says] (Melachim 1, 5:28):
". . . a month they were in Lebanon, [and] two months
at home." (Jerusalem Talmud, *Ketubot* 5:7)
       Pnei Moshe: They were only allowed to be in Leba-
non one month whereas they were in their homes two
months.

Rava said: When a man is led in for judgment [on the
Day of Judgment], he is asked: . . . did you engage in
procreation? (*Shabbat* 31a)

"I have lived with Lavan" (Bereshit 32:5):
       Rashi: [the word] *garti* ("I have lived") is numeri-
cally equal [and can be anagrammed] to 613 [the number of biblical *mitzvot*]: that is, I have lived with the
wicked Lavan and I have guarded the 613 commandments. . . .
       Birkat Eliyahu: for the commandment of procre-
ation[1] is equal [in importance] to all 613 commandments.

But that's not all. Many people uncritically and unques-
tioningly identify as "Jewish" the notion that the *sole* reason
the Creator instilled within humanity a desire for sexual intimacy was to ensure the propagation of the human race. Hence,
they maintain, the Torah laws that allow and promote marital intimacy do so *only* in order to encourage a high Jewish
birthrate. Any other use of intimacy (which does not lead, or

at least have the potential to lead, to pregnancy) is degraded and corrupt since sex is itself, by definition, inherently evil and degraded. The only redeeming quality of sexual intimacy is that it ensures the propagation of the human race. Accordingly, the Torah's permission of marital intimacy is, at best, an uneasy compromise with sex, and, consequently, is carefully circumscribed. Even as the Torah permits marital intimacy as inevitable and necessary, it disdains it. This antipathy is expressed, for example, through the Torah's stringent *Niddah* laws, which significantly restrict sexual contact between husband and wife. Similarly, the halakhic laws that regulate marital intimacy seek, as much as possible, to minimize and direct attention away from the enjoyment of the sexual act itself.

This line of thinking is patently false and fundamentally non-Jewish. Although procreation is an important reason for the Creator's design of sex and the Torah's permission and encouragement of marital intimacy, still it is *not* the *only* reason for His design of intimacy, and this contention fails to explain or account for much of the body of *halakhah* and the many statements found in the Written and Oral Torahs on the subject of marital intimacy. Indeed, it is refuted by these sources. The *halakhah*, for example, guards and protects, with no less vigor or zeal, a woman's right to sexual satisfaction in situations where pregnancy is clearly not an objective or a possible outcome. A pregnant woman, a nursing woman, and a woman physically incapable of conceiving (a woman past child-bearing years or otherwise physically unable to conceive) are all afforded the *exact* same protection by the Torah as the fertile woman whose potential to conceive is at a maximum; *the husband's halakhic obligation in any of these cases to satisfy his wife's desires for intimacy is exactly the same.*

A man must perform the *mitzvah* of *Onah* even when his wife is pregnant or nursing [and there is no possibility of pregnancy]. (Magen Avraham on *Shulchan Aruch, Orach Chaim* 240:1)

The *mitzvah* of *Onah* is not dependent on the possibility of conceiving because it is, rather, one of the obligations that a man has to his wife in order that she derive pleasure and not endure sorrow or suffering—comparable to the other obligations a husband has to his wife—i.e., to provide her with food and clothing . . . Therefore, even the husband of a pregnant woman, an old woman, or a barren woman is obligated to observe the same *mitzvah* of *Onah*. (*Igrot Moshe, Even HaEzer,* pt. 1, chap. 102)

המבטל [עונה] בזמן עיבורה כשלא מחלה האשה מחילה אמיתית בלב שלם
הוא חוטא גמור.

One who nullifies the *mitzvah* of *Onah* when his wife is pregnant—when she has not truly and wholeheartedly decided to temporarily forgo—is a complete sinner. (Y. Y. Kanievsky, the Steipler Gaon)

In the next chapter we will explore another, no less important, way in which the Torah enlists and harnesses sexual desire in the service of moral, Godly living.

6

The Torah's Encouragement of Sexual Enjoyment

R. MEIR'S QUESTION

What is the Torah's attitude regarding the enjoyment of marital intimacy? The answer to this question is derived from a remarkable passage in *Niddah* (31b) in which R. Meir entertains the question "Why did the Torah decree a seven-day *Niddah* period?" Why, R. Meir wonders, did God create the institution of *Niddah*? Why did the Creator design such an elaborate system—the complex, intricate, enormous body of Jewish law that governs the separation during menstruation and the subsequent reunion[1] of husband and wife? It is an astonishing question, and the answer R. Meir provides is no less astounding. R. Meir answers:

> . . . Because if he gets used to her through constant contact, he might become disgusted with her. Thus, the

Torah said, let her be *t'maiah* [and, hence, separated] for seven days so that she will be as beloved to her husband as she was when she entered the *chupah*.

The reason,[2] R. Meir explains, for the Almighty's creation of the elaborate institution of *Niddah* with its myriad *halakhot* is, *not* the Torah's desire to restrict a couple's ability to be intimate with each other, as many mistakenly believe, but, rather, just the opposite—the Torah's desire to *increase* the love of husband for wife, and wife for husband.

By limiting (*not* eliminating) and regulating the amount and times when husband and wife can share physical intimacy, the Torah fans the flames of desire between husband and wife such that, at every monthly reunion, the joy of intimacy resembles even that felt on the wedding day itself, many years ago. The laws of *Niddah*, calling as they do for periodic separation and abstention, protect a couple from the overindulgence and overfamiliarity that quickly lead to jading, dissatisfaction, disgust, and restlessness.

The implication of R. Meir's statement is clear: The Torah wants to increase love between husband and wife. The purpose of *Niddah*, according to R. Meir, is to enhance and rejuvenate the marital relationship.

If even the laws of *Niddah*, which *prohibit* marital relations, have as their ultimate goal to induce intimacy and increase the pleasure of intimacy shared by husband and wife, then how much more so must the laws which surround the performance of marital intimacy (the *mitzvah* of *Onah*) have as their objective the production and enjoyment of this intimacy! Indeed, the laws of *Niddah*, according to R. Meir's perspective, only find their ultimate fulfillment in the actual monthly intimate reunion of husband and wife. Otherwise, without this successful reunion, the *Niddah* laws are incomplete, their potential unrealized, their purpose subverted and frustrated, their promise stillborn. R. Zerach Eidelitz, student of R. Yonaton Eibeschitz and author of "*Or LaYesharim*," alluded to the interdependence between these two bodies of *halakhah*, their unity of design and purpose, when he wrote:

> Just as one must be well-versed in the laws of *Niddah*, so, too, one must be fluent in the laws of *Onah* (laws regulating performing marital intimacy). There is nothing blemished, shameful, or ugly, God forbid—there is only holiness and purity, when intimacy is performed properly.

Meticulous observance of *Niddah* finds its purpose and completion in the exuberant observance of *Onah*, and the enjoyment derived from the experience of marital intimacy is heightened and magnified immeasurably by the abstinence and refrain that *Niddah* requires.

CREATING *DEVEK*

One difficulty remains in our understanding of R. Meir's thesis. We understand that the institution of *Niddah*, with its usual twelve-day[3] separation period, creates a longing and a desire that culminates in the experience of the monthly "honeymoon." But R. Meir did *not* say "so there will be the same sexual passion and desire as when they went to the *Chupah*." Instead, he recalls the *love* of that first wedding day ("So that she will be as *beloved* to him as she was when she entered the *Chupah*"). In our discussion of R. Meir's statement so far, we have used the two concepts—love and longing— interchangeably. But are they interchangeable? What is the connection between the pleasure of physical union and the emotion of love? What is this identity that R. Meir takes for granted in the formulation of his answer?

In order to answer this question, it is important first to understand that the Torah wants to create the most intense, close, and loving relationship possible between husband and wife. The Torah's objective is to maximize intimacy—emotional, spiritual, and psychological intimacy. The term for this most intimate relationship between a couple is "*devek*" (lit., union, attachment). The Torah commands: "Therefore, a man shall leave his father and mother and cling ('*davak*') to his wife" (*Bereshit* 2:24). (See Ramban's commentary on *Chumash* for an explanation of this verse.)

> "This time . . ." (*Bereshit* 2:23): and this time only. Adam knew that he loved Chava immediately—automatically—without any preparation or effort by virtue of having been created as one being,[4] but he knew that, henceforth, it would not be thus [for other people]; rather, *it is only the active effort of devek between husband and wife that brings them closer together such that they become one.* (Netziv, *HaEmek Davar, Bereshit* 2:23)

How does one create *devek*? Rashi, commenting on the Talmud (*Sanhedrin* 58a–b), provides a simple formula: from pleasure comes *devek*. Rashi explains, "[If] she does not derive pleasure from the sexual intimacy, she does not cleave to him," from which we can infer that if she does derive pleasure from the sexual intimacy, she will cleave to him.

Now we can understand some more of the intent behind R. Meir's statement. The institution of *Niddah* (along with and through its counterpart and complement, marital intimacy) maximizes the pleasure to be had from the monthly reunion, and *this pleasure is the vehicle* for the creation of *devek*, the insoluble glue that binds husband and wife together.

The pleasure–*devek* relationship, it should be noted, is directly proportional—that is, the more pleasure, the more potential for *devek*. The Torah's goal is to maximize *devek*. Hence, the contention that the Torah tries to minimize or decrease the pleasure of marital intimacy could not be more incorrect.

Marital intimacy that produces an enormous amount of physical pleasure—*all* of which gets converted directly into *devek* (increased marital love and unity)—is celebrated in countless statements of the Sages.

> When a man unites with his wife in holiness[5]—the *Shechinah* dwells among them. (Ramban, based on *Sotah* 17a)

> If the intimacy is not amidst an abundance of love and desire, then the *Shechinah* will *not* dwell among them during intimacy. (Ramban)

Note that this pleasure is a vehicle, a means, to a greater, enviable, glorious end (the strengthening, reinforcement, and revitalization of the marriage bond), and *not* an end in itself. Intimacy performed *for its own sake* (solely for the production and enjoyment of the incomparable physical pleasure it affords, without thought or intention of achieving greater marital bonding) is frowned upon by the Torah and does *not* enjoy the Torah's encouragement. This type of hedonism and/or selfishness in sexual indulgence runs contrary to the Torah's entire conception of sexual enjoyment and is the basis for the Torah's denunciation and condemnation of the so-called "nine *Middot*," as we shall see. Many of the statements by our Sages which are, or appear to be, disapproving of the satisfaction of sexual desire refer to just this type of hedonistic and/or selfish "dead-end" pleasure, when the act of intimacy has been dissociated from its noble, spiritual goal of creating *devek*.

> Intimacy should not be performed as animals do, *solely* for the physical pleasure it affords. (Y. Luria, *the Holy Ari*)

Given this crucial distinction, we can, perhaps, understand the intent behind the following statement by Rabeinu Yaakov, the medieval author of the definitive halakhic code, the *Tur*:

> When he is intimate with her, his intent should not be on his own pleasure, but, rather, he should be as one honoring an obligation to another. . . . (*Tur, Orach Chaim* 240)

There is a fundamental, irreconcilable difference between the nature and quality of intimacy performed "for his own pleasure" and intimacy performed as "honoring an obligation to another." In the former, the emphasis is on oneself; in the latter, the concern is for another. In the former, intimacy is an exercise in greedy self-interest and gratification; in the latter, it is a glorious opportunity for selfless concern and altruistic benevolence. In the former, he is a taker; in the latter, he is a giver.

This is not to say, of course, that he should not enjoy intimacy. Instead, the intent is that he should not concentrate primarily on his own wants and desires; rather, his primary focus should be on his wife and her satisfaction.

Understandably, the quality of intimacy in the two cases contrasted cannot be compared. The Torah is not interested in halfway measures. A minimal experience of intimacy is insufficient. A grudging gift to a wife will not create *devek*, will not bind husband and wife together—just the opposite.

R. Y. Abuhav clarifies the intent behind the Tur's ruling when he writes,

> He should not have intimacy in order *only* to satisfy his own desires, but, rather, to satisfy [both his and] *also* his wife's desires. (*Menorat HaMaor* 185)

Similarly, R. Eliyahu, the Vilna Gaon, in his commentary to *Shulchan Aruch, Even HaEzer* 25, explains that the phrase "his intent should not be on his own pleasure" means that a husband should not be intimate with his wife solely for his own pleasure, without regard for his wife.

THE NINE *MIDDOT* (CHARACTERISTICS)

"And I will take out from among you those who rebel against Me and sin against Me" (*Yechezkel* 20:38): R. Levi said: These are the children of the "nine *Middot* (characteristics)."

Ran: Because there is an aspect of offence in their creation, the *children* will be rebels and sinners.

Sheeta Mekubetzet: *He* [himself] is rebellious and sinful to be intimate with his wife in an inappropriate and uncivilized way.

Though every person has free will, and no person is a prisoner of a predetermined, inevitable, or inescapable destiny, the parents' state of mind during intimacy does create fundamental character tendencies within the soul of the child born of that union. In *Nedarim* 20b, the Talmud enumerates nine types of sexual union, the offspring of which, the Talmud cautions, will be spiritually stunted and blemished. Remaining loyal to the Almighty and His Torah will be unusually difficult and demanding. These so-called "nine *Middot*" are:

1. בני אנוסה "Children of a Forced Partner"

Ravad: It goes without saying that this applies to one who had raped a woman and produced a child from her, but it also applies to his own wife. . . .

R. Yeshaya A. Z. Margaliot: Even if she is unwilling to have intimacy simply because she is temporarily angry with him or she happens not to be inclined at that time to have intimacy, he must not force her and have intercourse with her against her will while she fears him . . . And even if, after having just had intercourse, he wants to have intercourse again and she is not agreeable to it, it is forbidden (see *Eruvin* 100b).

Magen Avraham: "Even if she is not actually forced, as long as she is not completely agreeable."

Rami b. Chami said in the name of R. Assi: It is *forbidden* for a husband to compel his wife to be intimate with him. (*Eruvin* 100b)

Meiri: Even if he intends to do a *mitzvah* [of *pru urvu* and/or *Onah*]

2. בני שנואה "Children of a Hated Partner"

Ravad: As it sounds, he hates her in his heart, even if he has no intention of divorcing her.

Maharsha: [Or she hates him,] because what difference does it make whether he hates her or she hates him, comparable to the "children of drunkenness" (in which case it doesn't matter which partner is drunk). [The Maharsha, therefore, includes בני מורדת (5b) in this category.]

3. בני נדוי "Children of Excommunication"

One spouse was under a ban of ostracism of the *Beit Din* or of a Torah Sage. A person who is under such a ban is forbidden to have any type of social interaction—including intercourse with his or her spouse.

The Rosh also includes in this category בני אבל ("children of mourning") because a mourner during the first week of mourning (the period known as *Shivah*) is also halakhically forbidden to engage in social interaction or have marital intimacy (*Shulchan Aruch, Yoreh De'ah* 383).

4. בני תמורה "Children of Exchange"

Rashi: . . . [we are referring to] one who thought he was with another woman, but it was actually his wife he was with. This union is close to being adulterous, because he *meant* to commit adultery.

5a. בני מריבה "Children of Quarrel"

Rashi: One who has intercourse while engaged in a quarrel.

Ran: Even though he does not [generally] hate her, but, because they were quarreling at the time [of intimacy], the union is blemished.

5b. בני מורדת "Children of a Rebellious Wife"

A rebellious wife is a woman who has declared her total antipathy for her husband and her general unwillingness to fulfill her marital responsibilities to him— (see *Shulchan Aruch, Even HaEzer* 77:2).

R. Margaliyot: . . . As long as she is not fully appeased and completely renounces her earlier rebellion. . . .

6. בני שכרות "Children of Drunkenness"

Rashi: One who has intercourse while drunk.

The reference is not to a partner who is slightly light-headed. "Drunk" in this context means to a point where thought processes are impaired, confused, and muddled. (See Mishnah Berurah 240:18)

The Ravan HaYarchi, in his commentary to Tractate *Kallah Rabbati* (chap. 1), also includes in this category בני שינה ("children of a sleeping partner") because intercourse when either of the two partners is asleep (actually asleep, and not just drowsy—see Tosafot on *Niddah* 12a) is also marked by this lack of awareness.

7. בני גרושת הלב "Children of a Woman Whose Husband Has Resolved to Divorce Her"

Ran: He had already resolved in his heart to divorce her.

Ravad: . . . even if he does not hate her at all, but for some reason decided to divorce her, and she does not know about it. Even in a situation where he still loves her, such as those whom the *Beit Din* compels to divorce in certain exceptional cases or circumstances (enumerated in *Ketubot* 7:10), he must not be intimate with her.

8. בני ערבוביא "Children of Mixture"

Ravad: One who thinks of another woman while being intimate with his wife. . . .

"You shall not go after your hearts and after your eyes" (*Bamidbar* 15:39): From here Rabbi Yehuda HaNasi learned: One should not drink from one cup and look at another cup.

Ran: While one is having relations with his wife, he should not think of another woman. . . . (*Nedarim* 20b)

This also applies to a woman who thinks of another man.

Bamidbar Rabba Naso 9:43: When a woman is intimate with her husband, and is having intercourse with him, and her heart is set on another man she had seen in passing—there is no greater adultery than this. . . .

9. בני חצופה "Children of a Shameless Woman"

Ran: A woman who is brazen in verbally demanding relations.

Ravad: [This applies only if she speaks in a brazen, insolent, shameless style.] But if she speaks in a proper way and she appeases him with words and adorns herself before him so that he should notice her in a sexual way—of that the Sages say (*Eruvin* 100b) that she will be rewarded with exceptional children, as Leah did and she produced Issachar (See *Bereshit* 30).

A woman can make a discreet, but suggestive, statement or indicate that she desires relations by dressing in a manner that will attract her husband. (R. Mordechai Eliyahu)

SANCTITY AND SEXUALITY

Why are these nine types of union so strongly denounced by the Torah as "sinful and rebellious"? What's wrong with these types of encounters?

> The essential sanctity of intimacy depends upon the intent of the partners during intimacy. (*Menorat HaMaor* 178)

All nine types of union share one common denominator, one common theme: in each case, the physical pleasure has been divested of the emotional or psychic component that would produce *devek*. This pleasure is incapable of producing *devek*: either it will not or it cannot. That is exactly what the Torah does not want.

> The essence of sanctification during intimacy, in fulfillment of the Torah's commandment "You shall be holy" (*VaYikra* 19:2), is to avoid the nine *Middot*. (Vilna Gaon, *Tikkunei HaZohar*, end of 53)

> The essential requirement for the sanctification of intimacy is to increase the love and the unity between husband and wife. (Vilna Gaon, quoted in *Mishkan Yisrael*, p. 45)

From the Vilna Gaon's explanation emerges a sublime, uniquely Jewish, definition of sanctity in one's sexual conduct. Sanctity is creating emotional union between husband and wife via their sexual relationship. The essence of the nine *Middot* is to prevent or avoid creating such emotional intimacy and bonding. Sanctity, says the Vilna Gaon, is avoiding the nine *Middot*; sanctity is ensuring that the pleasure from every marital encounter is converted into *devek*, into further strengthening, solidifying, and cementing the marital bond.

And a Jew must attain sanctity in this area as he must in all other areas.

> A person must make himself holy during marital intimacy. . . . (*Zohar, Midrash HaNe'elam, Bereshit*, "Toztai ha'aretz nefesh chayah")

It is clear, then, that attaining holiness in marital intimacy does *not* require minimizing the pleasure of intimacy. On the contrary: sexual sanctity, transforming the experience from a physical act of selfish sexual self-gratification to a spiritual act of selfless concern and consideration, is best obtained through maximizing the pleasure of his or her spouse during intimacy.

> The other person's physical needs ("*goshmiyut*") are my spiritual concerns ("*ruchniyut*"). (R. Yisroel Salanter)

With the Vilna Gaon's astonishing definition of holiness, we can better understand many statements of the talmudic Sages and the Rishonim, the great talmudic commentators.

"COMPLETE" INTIMACY

Rashi (*Nedarim* 20b) speaks repeatedly of "complete intercourse," in contrast to "plain" or "illicit" intercourse. The first is good, Rashi explains; the second is not. What's the difference?

"Complete" intercourse refers to physical intimacy that will lead to the strengthening of emotional bonds between husband and wife. "Plain" or "illicit" intercourse is physical intimacy devoid or divested of that all-important emotional component; it is physical intimacy, sex, for its own sake.

The Ramban elaborates on this distinction in his unique explanation of the biblical verse (*Shmot* 21:10) "ועונתה לא יגרע שארה כסותה." This verse is usually translated as ". . . he may not diminish her allowance ('*shearah*'), clothing ('*k'sutah*'), or conjugal rights ('*onatah*')". The Ramban, however, understands the verse differently. He explains that all three refer to one and the same marital obligation: a husband's responsibility to create an ambiance for marital intimacy rich in emotional intimacy.

> Her physical intimacy ("*kiruv basar*"—the Sages say this is the meaning of "*shearah*"), the cover of her bed ("*k'sutah*"), and her time of love ("*onatah*") he may not withhold from her, for this is the "manner of daughters" (see verse). The reason [for this threefold commandment] is to ensure that he not lie with her as if by chance and on the ground, as one has intercourse with a prostitute, whereas another wife reposes in a bed of honor in which husband and wife are "as one flesh." Therefore, the Torah prevented this from happening.

All of these elements together, the Ramban explains, are features of marital intimacy which possesses the full emotional component and ability to strengthen the marital relationship. This, according to the Ramban, is the intimacy the Torah desires and approves of. The Torah disapproves of intimacy devoid of this component; the Ramban compares such sexual encounters to "a chance encounter, as if one were engaged in an act of prostitution" because it is a sexual act for its own sake, in order only to satisfy his desires. Only the two together—passionate sexual desire and emotional intimacy—satisfies the Torah's conception of sanctified marital intimacy.

Armed with this definition of sanctifying sexual behavior, we can readily identify the failing in each of the nine *Middot*.

1. בני אנוסה "Children of a Forced Partner"

Clearly, this brutal act of violation—either physical or psychological—does not inspire love or respect in a wife who fearfully or helplessly succumbs to her husband's advances, nor does it inspire concern or consideration in the husband who selfishly, savagely conscripts his wife into his service. The physical act is bereft of any subtle, tender emotion uniting husband and wife.

2. בני שנואה "Children of a Hated Partner"

Ravad: This union is blemished because it is like illicit intercourse, not like marital intercourse.

Because he hates his wife, it is inevitable, Rashi explains, that

His heart is on another woman during intercourse; and the Sages said that when he has intercourse with her, it is not considered a complete sexual act because he hates her so, rather it is merely an act of illicit intercourse.

Similarly, the Ran comments:

Because he hates her, he thinks of another woman.

3. בני נדוי "Children of Excommunication"

(Rosh: בני אבל ("Children of Mourning")

In these situations, his mind is otherwise engaged, riveted by the searing tragedy confronting him. His emotions are shattered. Both these situations inspire a lonely, debilitating sense of isolation. He is incapable of building up a relationship, of reaching out emotionally to his spouse.

4. בני תמורה "Children of Exchange"

This intimacy does nothing to enhance the marital relationship. The pleasure resulting from this intimacy does not produce *devek*; on the contrary, it drives the couple further apart.

5a. בני מריבה "Children of Quarrel"

Ran: Even though he does not [generally] hate her, but, because they were quarreling at the time, the union is blemished.

Ravad: This intimacy is like illicit prostitution, since it is not amidst love.

An emotional bond between husband and wife does exist. However, since, at the time of intimacy, that bond had been relaxed or weakened and, as a result, they were not concentrating on strengthening that bond, this particular encounter has done nothing to promote that emotional relationship and is nothing more than a physical encounter.

5b. בני מורדת "Children of a Rebellious Wife"

R. Margaliot: . . . As long as she is not fully appeased and completely renounces her earlier rebellion, the sexual act is like prostitution because it does not come from love.

6. בני שכרות "Children of Drunkenness"

(Ravan: בני שינה ("Children of a Sleeping Partner")

Rosh: When he or she is drunk, they are not completely intent on what they are doing.

Ravad: For they have no intention of love.

Ran : Because he is drunk, he cannot concentrate on his wife.

In such a union, the emotional component simply *cannot* be present because at least one spouse lacks the awareness and clarity of thought needed to elevate it above and beyond a mere physical act and endow it with any greater significance. Rashi comments:

For the sexual act he is involved in is not considered a complete one, but, rather, an act of illicit prostitution, whereby he intends only to commit a sexual act per se, [the partner's identity being irrelevant].

The Talmud (*Niddah* 17a) praised the Royal House of Munbaz (of Adiabene, converts to Judaism) for three singular practices, one of which was their practice of performing marital intimacy during the day. But, the Talmud asks, isn't that counter to the *halakhah* taught by Rav Huna that Jews, owing to their great modesty, do *not* perform marital intimacy during the day? The

Talmud explains why their behavior, seemingly at odds
with halakhic practice, was praiseworthy. The members
of the Royal House were intimate during the day rather
than at night because of their fear that, at night:

> Sleep overtakes him, she becomes undesirable to
> him and his heart rejects her.[6] (*Niddah* 17a)

Rashi explains:

> Because he is overcome by sleep, he does not fully
> desire her and has intercourse *merely* for the pur-
> pose of observing the *mitzvah* of *Onah* or in order
> to please her, and his heart recoils from her. This
> is one of the "nine *Middot*."

The significance of this explanation cannot be overstated.
According to Rashi, not only is marital intimacy that is
performed "merely" to observe the *mitzvah* of *Onah*
inadequate; it is condemned as one of the nine *Middot*.
Such a union is forbidden. One could mistakenly enter-
tain the notion that this is, in fact, the highest level, the
choicest condition, in which to perform the *mitzvah* of
Onah—that is, solely with the intent to perform a *mitzvah*,
free of the taint of sexual desire or passion. Not so, explains Rashi. This is far from desirable; in fact, it is completely unacceptable. Marital intimacy is praiseworthy
when it is amidst desire, desire of each spouse for the
other. This is the intent behind, and fulfillment of,
the statement "I created the *Yetzer Hara*, and I created
the Torah as its spice." Intimacy without the infusion of
strong passionate desire, with only a halfhearted, un-
enthusiastic commitment to fulfill a *mitzvah*, is *not* the
intimacy the Almighty approves of. This marital intimacy
does not enjoy His favor and encouragement.[7]

If the intimacy is *not* amidst an abundance of love and desire, then the *Shechinah* will *not* dwell among them during intimacy. (Ramban)

During intimacy, he can talk with her about intimate matters in order to increase his desire for her.[8] (*Tur, Orach Chaim* 240)

There is no good in being intimate without desire; on the contrary, it is necessary that he have desire. (R. Yosef Chaim of Baghdad ["Ben Ish Chai"], *Torah Lishmah, Orach Chaim* 72)

7. בני גרושת הלב "Children of a Woman Whose Husband Has Resolved to Divorce Her"

Intimacy on his part is intimacy for its own sake, without intent to strengthen the permanence of the marital bond. This intimacy cannot create long-term *devek*.

Rosh: And even if he does not hate her, for once he is set on divorcing her, he [inevitably] thinks of another woman.

8. בני ערבוביא "Children of Mixture"

This case is similar to the בני תמורה case (#4) discussed above. Obviously, this intimacy does nothing to enhance the marital relationship because such intimacy lacks any emotional focus on the spouse. The pleasure resulting from this intimacy has been diverted away from the spouse and misdirected towards another person. Such intimacy does not produce *devek*, but, rather, destroys whatever *devek* already existed.

9. בני חצופה "Children of a Shameless Woman"

The deficiency here would seem to be that the intimacy is characterized by a lack of respect in three dimensions. One who initiates a request for intimacy in a coarse, brazen manner betrays a lack of respect for her [or his] spouse as well as a denial of the sanctity of intimacy itself. Such undignified behavior, in turn, inspires an attitude of disdain in the spouse and ruins, from the start, any possibility for either spouse of an emotional component rich in respect or consideration.

Marital intimacy is an integral part of a Jew's life, and a Jew must attain holiness in this arena as in all others. As the Vilna Gaon explained, sanctity is attained by avoiding the nine *Middot*—that is, by ensuring that both husband and wife emerge from *every* marital encounter renewed and rejuvenated. This requires that intimacy be "complete"—that is, enthusiastic, not halfhearted or dispassionate. Sexual sanctity is attained, *not* by minimizing sexual desire, but, rather, by maximizing desire for one's spouse *exclusively*, and converting the pleasure that results into *devek* for one's spouse.

The letter ט[9] [of *Dvarim* 5:16, the commandment to honor one's father and mother in the restatement of the ten Commandments] has crowns on it [in an original Torah scroll] because . . . father and mother are warned to avoid the nine *Middot* enumerated in Tractate *Nedarim*. . . ." (Rabeinu Yaakov, *Ba'al HaTurim* on the Torah, *Dvarim* 5:16)

The connection would seem to be: If a husband and wife sanctify themselves in intimacy by carefully avoiding the nine

Middot, then the child born of their union will, according to the Talmud in Tractate *Nedarim*, possess a pure, unblemished soul and will, with relative ease, become righteous. This righteous child will observe the Almighty's Torah and fulfill its commandments, prominent among them the commandment to honor one's father and mother. This, perhaps, is Rabeinu Yaakov's message: if a husband and wife take great care to avoid the nine *Middot*, they will merit children who will honor them in fulfillment of the Torah's commandment to "honor your father and mother."

> One who scrupulously observes the details of the laws regarding intimacy outlined in chapter 240 of the Orach Chaim section of Shulchan Aruch will merit children who will scrupulously fulfill the details of the laws regarding honoring one's parents outlined in chapter 240 of the Yoreh Deah section of Shulchan Aruch. (Yeshaya A. Z. Margaliyot, *Da'at HaKedushah*, p. 12)

> In the section of the Torah in which God gives Avraham Avinu the *mitzvah* of *Brit Milah* (*Bereshit* 17:1–27), all the letters of the Hebrew alphabet appear except one— the letter ט. Similarly, when the Torah describes the small, fledgling Jewish nation that descended to Egypt (*Bereshit* 46:8–27), the letter ט does not appear in any of the names of the seventy members of Yaakov's family [to emphasize the unadulterated excellence and holiness of the entire Jewish nation]. Said God to Avraham: "I established a covenant with you to be God to you and to your descendants—avoid the nine *Middot*!" Similarly, there is no ט in the first statement of the ten Commandments (*Shmot* 20:2–14) because sanctity in sexual matters is as important as all of the ten

Commandments together. (Rokeach on the Torah, *Lech Lecha*, p. 30)

We will close this chapter with a sampling of quotes that describe the holy variety of marital intimacy which, in marked contrast to the nine *Middot* presented above, enjoys the Torah's full enthusiastic encouragement.

Her desire should be directed at him, [so] that there should be no disagreement or lack of harmony between them, but, rather, [there should be] "love and companionship, peace and deep friendship." (*Reishit Chochmah*, *Shaar HaKedushah*, chap. 16)

The important thing is that he engage in the marital act with love and affection, when she desires it and he is thinking about her and intending to fulfill the commandment. (R. Moshe HaMakiri, *Seder HaYom*)

In the next chapter, we will describe how the *mitzvah* of *Onah* transforms marital intimacy from "plain intimacy" to "complete intimacy."

7

The *Mitzvah* of *Onah*

There is a biblical commandment addressed to a husband to be sexually intimate with his wife. This *mitzvah*, the *mitzvah* of *Onah*, is one of the 613 biblical commandments. The biblical source for this *mitzvah* is the verse in *Shmot* (21:10): "He shall not diminish her conjugal rights."[1] Significantly, there is no reciprocal obligation addressed to a wife.

R. Yaakov Y. Kanievsky, the Steipler Gaon, described the *mitzvah* of *Onah* this way: עונה היא מצות עשה דאורייתא כאכילת מצה, ‎ . . . והמבטלה הרי זה עבירה גמורה. "*Onah* is a positive *mitzvah* of the Torah no less than the positive *mitzvah* of the Torah to eat *matzah* on Pesach night."

> Rava said: A man must please his wife with intimacy. (*Pesachim* 72b)

> And if . . . he realizes that she is enticing him and trying to please him and adorning herself for him so that he should notice her—he must approach her sexually. (*Shulchan Aruch, Orach Chaim* 240:1)

I have heard from one of the giants of the generation that if a woman shows signs of interest, and demonstrates affection for her husband, then this is the true *Onah* that the Torah refers to (and the husband is obliged to be intimate with her). (R' Chaim Dovid Azulai, *Mahrit HaAyin* on *Niddah* 31)

The main *mitzvah* of *Onah* is when the husband sees that his wife desires to be intimate with him . . . This obligation is a full Torah obligation . . . Our Sages explained the verse "and he may not diminish her conjugal rights" to mean that he is required to please his wife when he sees that she desires him. (*Igrot Moshe*, *Even HaEzer* pt. 3, chap. 28)

What does the observance of the *mitzvah* of *Onah* entail? What must a husband do in order to fulfill the halakhic requirements of this *mitzvah*?

The parameters of the *mitzvah* of *Onah* that the Sages established are designed to satisfy the wife's desire. (Ravad)

In general terms, the *mitzvah* of *Onah* requires that a husband satisfy his wife's needs, both physical and emotional, for intimacy.

A husband fulfills the *mitzvah* of *Onah* when he shows his wife that he loves and desires her, and that he wants to please her.[2]

Understandably, the manner of fulfilling this *mitzvah* is a highly individualized process, and very much a function of each woman's unique personality and needs. A husband is required *by Torah law* to learn, know, and do what will give his wife sexual pleasure. This learning process takes time,

consideration, devotion, humility, honesty, and a fair amount
of humor. Knowledge of a wife's personal tastes—in all matters, not just in matters of intimacy—is so important to the
long-term success of a marriage that the Torah calls on the
husband to devote the entire first year of marriage, free of any
and all distractions, to its acquisition.

> When a man takes a new wife, he shall not go out in
> the army, neither shall he be charged with anything, he
> shall be free for his home for one year and shall make
> the wife he had taken happy. (*Dvarim* 24:5)

> In order to familiarize himself with her, and to attach
> his good will to her, and to introduce into his heart her
> image and all her actions. . . (*Sefer HaChinuch* #582)

> In the first year of marriage . . . effort should be made
> for the union of (husband and wife), for that is the intent
> of creation: "and they shall be one flesh." (*Letters of
> Chazon Ish*, #1)

THE *MITZVAH* OF *ONAH* IS INCUMBENT
UPON THE HUSBAND

Why is the *mitzvah* of *Onah* directed solely at a husband? Why
is there no comparable *mitzvah* incumbent upon a wife? We
will suggest two reasons:

1. A man, by nature, is not embarrassed to approach his
wife. It is not in the nature of a woman, in contrast, to make
overt overtures; instead, she attempts to gain her husband's
attention and interest through more subtle, delicate means—
by making herself appear attractive, etc. The Torah, solicitous/
protective of a wife's honor and dignity, formalized an obli-

gation on a husband to look for, understand, and respond to such "signals" sent by his wife. The Torah highly values modesty and discretion in a Jewish woman, and the *mitzvah* of *Onah* (which requires a husband to be aware of, and attentive to, his wife's needs and desires) ensures that the wife's needs and desires will not be ignored or overlooked as a result of her dignified, reserved behavior.

> The Sages established the *Onah* requirements (in *Ketubot* 61b) because of the woman's natural modesty and shyness. (*Igrot Moshe, Even HaEzer* 3:28)

> R. Shmuel b. Nachmani said in the name of R. Yochanan: Any woman who solicits her husband to marital intimacy will have children the likes of whom did not exist even in the generation of Moshe. [Regarding the members of Moshe's generation the Torah specifically omits the praise "discerning" (compare verses 13 and 15 in chapter 1 of *Dvarim*); regarding the family of Yissachar (the child of Leah, who invited her husband Yaakov to be intimate with her (*Bereshit* 30:16), from which union Yissachar was born), the Bible specifically describes them as "discerning" (*Divrei HaYamim* 1, 12:33).]

> Is that right? Did not R. Yitzchak b. Avdimi say: ". . . a wife solicits with her heart; a husband does so with his mouth—this is a fine character trait among women"?

> R. Shmuel b. Nachmani citing R. Yochanan meant that she behaves lovingly to him. [From this loving behavior, he understands that she desires to be intimate with him, and he satisfies this desire. This, according to R. Yochanan, is the most desirable manner in which to initiate marital intimacy.]

> Rashi: "She behaves lovingly": She shows him signs of affection. (*Eruvin* 100b)

Rashi: "She behaves lovingly:" She does not demand intimacy explicitly, but, rather, she shows him through her words that she desires to be intimate with him, as Leah [did when she invited Yaakov into her tent], for from that union came exceptional offspring. (*Nedarim* 20)

Ran: "She behaves lovingly:" She invites him with appeasing words and behavior, like Leah who only invited Yaakov into her tent but did not explicitly, verbally demand intimacy from him. (*Nedarim* 20)

The main *mitzvah* of *Onah* is when he *sees* . . . and he understands. . . . (*Chochmat Adam* 128:19)

This feature of the *mitzvah* of *Onah* (the obligation placed upon a husband to be alert to any indication or nuance from his wife that she desires intimacy) is, of course, intended to aid and benefit a woman—not to thwart her or prevent her from communicating her desire for intimacy. Accordingly, in such cases, for example, where a husband fails to correctly discern and decipher the signals that have been sent his way, a wife is allowed to express, openly and modestly, her request for intimacy.

This is the healthy situation: that the husband understands from his wife's intimations of affection [that she wants to be intimate, and he responds accordingly]. But if he does not understand [these subtle signs], certainly the wife can openly express her desire for intimacy: Because that which is written about her not openly demanding intimacy is not a law, but, rather, a proper practice. Therefore, if the husband does not understand the intimation, then certainly she can speak to him directly; and she should say it as modestly as possible. . . . (R. Aviner, *Etzem MeAtzmy*)

It is a grievous crime to withhold intimacy from a wife who has discreetly and modestly intimated her desire for her husband's attention, and the Rabbis are unequivocal and unreserved in their condemnation of a husband guilty of such cruelty or neglect.

> R. Yehoshua b. Levi said: Any man who knows his wife to be a righteous woman and does not visit her [when he sees that she has a need for intimacy—Ravad] is called a sinner. . . . (*Yevamot* 62b)

> "If you should afflict my daughters" (*Bereshit* 31:50): If you afflict them by withholding intimacy. (*Yoma* 77a–b)
> Rashi: By withholding their [right to] marital intimacy.

> It is forbidden for a man to refrain from satisfying his wife's needs for intimacy. And if he transgressed and refrained *in order to afflict* her[3]—he has transgressed a Torah prohibition, as it says ". . . he may not diminish her allowance, clothing, or conjugal rights" (*Shmot* 21:10). (Rambam, *Hilchot Ishut* 14:7)

Similarly, it is forbidden for a woman to withhold intimacy from her husband.

> . . . [T]hey are formally obligated to each other in matters of intimacy, since they married each other for this reason. On his part, beside this formal obligation, he is subject to the *mitzvah* of *Onah*; on her part, in contrast, she is not subject to the *mitzvah* of *Onah*, but she is formally obligated to him. (Rashba, *Nedarim* 15b)

> A woman [who is permitted to immerse in the *mikveh*] must not refrain from doing so. (Jerusalem Talmud, *Niddah* 7b)

It is a sin for a woman to delay immersing in the *mikveh*
in order to afflict her husband. . . . (Beit Yosef to *Tur Yoreh
Deah* 197)

2. The primary enjoyment by a man of intimacy is the
activity of physical intimacy and intercourse. The same, perhaps, cannot be said for a woman. While a woman also derives
enjoyment from the physical experience, her primary enjoyment is the emotional intimacy she shares with her husband.[4]
Without the emotional component, her physical experience is
not optimal. A man does not tend to need the emotional build-
up that is the essential feature of foreplay. A woman does. The
two processes—emotional and physical—are inextricably
bound up for a woman. A husband satisfies his wife's desire
initially by focusing on her emotional needs. The physical consummation follows inevitably as a natural corollary. A man can
become sexually aroused in an instant and be fully prepared
for intercourse without preliminaries or preparations; similarly,
when intercourse is complete, a man can just as quickly lose
all sexual desire. Not so a woman. A woman, slowly and steadily,
"climbs an emotional mountain" before she reaches the sum-
mit and fully desires physical consummation of intimacy. So,
too, on the "way down," after physical intimacy has ended—
the woman must make the slow steady descent back down from
the heights of sexual excitement and passion. If intercourse
occurs before the wife is ready, then intimacy is, for her, an
experience of exploitation and resentment rather than a pleasurable expression of her husband's love. Similarly, if a husband, his needs satisfied, selfishly turns away from his wife and
neglects to escort her gently and lovingly down the emotional
mountain, then marital intimacy is, for her, an experience of
frustration and rage.

It was taught, R. Meir used to say: Whoever marries his
daughter to a boor is as though he bound and laid her
before a lion; just as a lion tears [his prey] and devours
it and has no shame, so a boor strikes[5] and cohabits and
has no shame. (*Pesachim* 49b)

Tosafot: Rabbenu Tam explained: Just as a lion
tears and eats and does not wait for its prey to die, so,
too, a boor does not wait until she is appeased.

"על פי דין תורה אסור לעשות הביאה באופן שהאשה אינה מפויסת, ומחויב
לפייסה בקירוב בחבוק ונשוק עד שתתאוה לחבור: דאם לא כן, הרי היא
כנתונה לפני ארי דורס ואוכל, כמבואר בפסים דף מ"ט . . . ועון פלילי
הוא לעשות מה שמגיע צער לאשתו. . . ."

According to Torah law, it is forbidden to be intimate
in such a way that she will not be pleased, and he is
obligated to appease her with closeness, kissing, and
hugging until she desires to consummate the intimacy:
for otherwise she is like one bound and laid before a
lion who tears and devours, as is explained in *Pesachim*
49 . . . and it is a criminal sin to do that which causes
anguish to his wife. . . . (Y. Y. Kanievsky)

"ומה שחוטף ובועל מיד בלא קירוב ופורש תיכף ומיד ומתרחק ממנה, הנה
הבעל חושב שעולה בזה מדריגות גדולות, באמת לא נגרש מתאוותו ויצרו
כלום, ויצרו שלו מפמים בהחלט בהנאה שלימה, אבל אשתו לא נהנית כלל
מהנהגת זאת ואדרבה היא כואבת ומבוישת ובמסתרים תבכה ודמעתה אינה
חוזרת דשער דמעות לא ננעלו."

When a man grabs and has intercourse immediately without any closeness, after which [his needs
satisfied] he separates immediately and distances himself from her—the husband [mistakenly] thinks that,
through this practice, he ascends to great spiritual
heights. In reality, his desires have in no way been di-
minished, and his drive is completely appeased with
complete satisfaction; but his wife has not received any
pleasure at all from this type of behavior—on the con-

trary, she is hurt and shamed, and she cries in secrecy and her tears do not go unanswered, for the "Gates of Tears" were never locked. (Y. Y. Kanievsky)

The Torah wants neither exploitation and resentment nor frustration and rage, so it legislated a formal Torah obligation (the *mitzvah* of *Onah*) on a husband to slowly, gently, and lovingly escort his wife up the mountain, and to continue the act of emotional intimacy long after intercourse is ended until the emotional descent is complete. The halakhic elements of *Onah* are essential in successfully accomplishing both tasks.

> R. Chiyya said: What is meant by the scriptural text (Job 35:11) "Who teaches us by the beasts of the earth and makes us wise by the fowls of the heaven"? . . .This refers to the rooster which first coaxes and then mates. R. Yochanan observed: If the Torah had not been given, we could have learned . . . proper conduct ("*derech eretz*") from the rooster who first coaxes and then mates. (*Eruvin* 100b)
>
> It is [a demonstration of] his love for her that he spreads his wings over her, just like a chicken spreads her wings over her chicks. (Maharal, *Netivot Olam*, vol. 2, *Netiv Hatziniyut*, end of ch. 1)

He should draw her heart with seductive, graceful words of love and desire until he binds her thoughts to his and she desires to have intercourse. (*Menorat HaMaor* 185)

Also *after intercourse* he should continue to chat lightly and lovingly with her in order that she not think that his whole intent in speaking this way earlier was for the sake of his own pleasure. Therefore, to counter this mistaken notion, he should continue to appease her even after intercourse. (*Damesek Eliezer*)

"כשמשתדלים לשמחה בשעת הביאה ולפניה ולאחריה, אין זה מגונה, ח"ו,
רק מצוה . . . [ו]משועבד לזה על פי הדין."

When he tries to make her happy during intimacy, as
well as before and after, there is nothing improper, God
forbid; there is only Mitzvah . . . and he is required to
do so according to Torah law. (Y. Y. Kanievsky)

In sum, we presented two reasons to explain why the
Torah's *mitzvah* of *Onah* is addressed only to a husband, and
with these two reasons we were able to account for many of
the halakhic elements of the *Mitzvah*:

1. A husband will, easily and without reservation or hesi-
tation, express his desire for intimacy; a woman, in contrast,
who tends to be more reserved and modest, will not. To ensure that a wife's needs will not be forgotten, the Torah legislated a formal obligation on a husband to be alert to any indication from his wife that she desires intimacy and to provide
her with that intimacy.

and

2. A husband does not tend to need the same emotional
preparation for intimacy that a wife does. The *mitzvah* of *Onah*
(through its elements of, for example, loving words, hugging
and kissing, and physical closeness) ensures that a husband
will create the atmosphere that will satisfy his wife's emotional,
as well as her physical, needs.

What should a man do in order to have prosperous
children blessed with longevity?
He should perform the desires of Heaven and the
desires of his wife.
These are "the desires of Heaven": . . . ; these are
"the desires of his wife":

R. Eliezer says: he should seduce her during intimacy [he should provide the emotional dimension of
intimacy described in Answer 2].

R. Yehudah says: he should gladden her with intimacy [when he sees that she desires intimacy] [he
should be alert and responsive to the subtle signs she
displays that indicate that she wants intimacy as described in Answer 1] (Tractate *Kallah*, ch. 1)

"MORE THAN MATERIAL WEALTH": THE *SOTAH*

The Talmud provides us with an invaluable general principle
regarding how to orchestrate proper Torah intimacy that is
pleasing to a woman. The Talmud entertains the question of a
husband who has an opportunity to change from being a don-
key driver (his profession when they married) to being a camel
driver. This latter profession, because it is more demanding
(involving far more distant journeys), is a much more lucrative
trade; his salary will be increased manyfold. Such a career
change will have another consequence: because this new profession is more physically taxing (requiring longer periods away
from home), it will affect profoundly their relationship. The
number of times they have marital intimacy will drop significantly. Can the husband change careers without his wife's consent? The Talmud concludes that the husband cannot change
careers without her consent because such a career change will
impact adversely on her. But she will be the recipient of all that
extra income? The Talmud (*Ketubot* 62b) concludes: "A woman
prefers one measure of prosperity as long as it is accompanied
by *intimate lightheartedness* to nine measures of material wealth
and abstinence."

Perhaps this consideration will account for the construction of *Mishnah* 3:4 in tractate *Sotah*. After describing the (usually immediate; in some cases, time-delayed) gruesome death throes of a woman whom the "*Sotah* waters" have pronounced guilty of adultery, the *Mishnah* quotes two statements by R. Yehoshua which, seemingly, have little to do with the discussion at hand:

1. A woman prefers one measure of prosperity as long as it is accompanied by intimate lightheartedness to nine measures of material wealth and abstinence.
2. A foolishly pious man; a cunning wicked man; a woman who pretends to be pious; and people who invest all their efforts in showy, but fundamentally meaningless displays of piety—all these people destroy the world.

At first glance, these ideas have little, if anything, to do with the subject of our *Mishnah*, which is the indictment and punishment of a *sotah*; we are at a loss to explain their inclusion in this *Mishnah*. What relevance do these ideas have here, in the climax of a series of *mishnayot* that describe the sequence of the trial and punishment of the guilty *sotah*? Is there no better place in the many *mishnayot* to record these very important observations? The main player in the *sotah* drama—the woman herself—certainly does not fit easily or naturally into any of the categories R. Yehoshua enumerated in his list of people who "destroy the world."

We can suggest that the author of the *Mishnah*, through his construction of the *Mishnah* (his juxtaposition of the grim fate of the *sotah* and these statements of R. Yehoshua), wishes to address an essential feature of the marriage relationship.

The loss or absence of this feature may ultimately be responsible for the disintegration of the marriage and the creation of a *sotah*.

We regard the *sotah* in her downfall; the *sotah* waters have revealed her guilt, and the punishment is absolute and unrelenting. No one can defend her unpardonable behavior; no one can excuse her unspeakable crime. And yet, as we consider her tragic fate, we can well wonder: what motivated this behavior? What inspired this extreme course of action?

As if in answer to this query, the *Mishnah* quotes R. Yehoshua's first statement to the effect that "more than a woman desires material wealth, she desires intimacy." A wife who is given the emotional intimacy she craves and needs by her husband, who is secure in the knowledge that her husband loves her, will not seek to derive intimacy from interaction with men other than her husband.

For even if the sotah *waters declare a woman innocent, all is not well with this marriage.* Many events preceded this day when the woman stands in the Temple courtyard and drinks the *sotah* waters. This woman had had overly friendly private interaction with another man. Her husband had expressed his displeasure over her improper friendliness with this man and had warned her not to continue with this course of behavior, and, despite her husband's express protestations and warning, this woman secreted herself with that selfsame strange man again. Although the *sotah* waters may vindicate her and reveal that she did not, in fact, have an adulterous physical affair with him, nevertheless she has shared a degree of emotional intimacy with this man that should have been reserved exclusively for her husband.

The husband who regards his *sotah* wife might well wonder what role he played in the genesis of this tragedy. (This is *not* to excuse, in any way, the *sotah*'s unpardonable offense. The Torah's prohibition against adultery is absolute under any and all conditions. Perhaps this is why the author of the *Mishnah* only offers this criticism *after* describing the horrible punishment of the adulteress wife.) He supported her financially; did he also support her emotionally? Did he provide her with the emotional reassurance and intimacy she needed, the reassurance and intimacy for which she married him in the first place?

Adam married Chava, and they began the population and settlement of the whole world. Every marriage is just as significant. The birth of every single Jewish child is so important that it is considered as if the parents have "built a full world" (Rambam, *Hilchot Ishut* 15:16). Consequently, the dissolution of a family, the disintegration of the marital relationship, is comparable in its tragic proportions to the destruction of a world.

Who destroyed this world? The woman's role in this tragedy is obvious; her duplicity has been revealed for all to see. But what of her husband?

He may seek to defend his behavior, and attempt to justify his emotional neglect of his wife. He may point with great justification and indignity to the many responsibilities and obligations he fulfills for his family. What time remains, he might ask in some exasperation, in which to discuss dresses and curtains and china patterns?

In response to this last objection, the *Mishnah* quotes R. Yehoshua's second statement. One of those who "destroys a world" is the foolishly pious man; another is the clever wicked man. The foolishly pious man, the Talmud explains, will not save a drowning woman because to do so would require that he touch her. Such unthinking, misguided "piety" is as destructive as the actions of the wicked man who shrewdly hides behind a facade of piety and rationalization. Either mode of behavior is catastrophic. What caused his neglect of his wife? Was it thoughtless, ill-reasoned oversight and carelessness ("foolish piety," which grabs the unimportant and dismisses the important)? Or was it due to cruel, uncaring, malicious neglect (the wicked, uncaring man who attempts to hide and justify his cruel behavior)? In the end, R. Yehoshua informs us, it does not really matter—either path is equally perilous and ultimately destructive.

The husband watches the punishment of his wayward wife, perhaps with some righteous indignation, but *his* crime is also reprehensible. Whether carelessly or cruelly, unthinkingly or indifferently, he neglected his wife and failed to provide her with the life-giving sustenance for which she married him.

> Reason dictates that a husband is obligated to provide his wife with intimacy: For "everyone knows why a bride enters the chupah" [that is, she marries in order to have someone with whom she can be intimate, see *Shabbat* 33a] and due to the fact that she has a husband she cannot obtain this intimacy anywhere else; therefore, if he withholds intimacy from his wife, he steals the pleasure that is rightfully hers . . . for she is not his captive such that he can withhold her pleasures from her. . . . (*Birkat HaNetziv* on *Mechilta* D'R. Yishmael, *Mishpatim* 3)

> [H]e is not allowed to steal his wife's Onah. . . . (*Noda B'Yehudah, Orach Chaim* 1:35)

A woman wants—*needs*—lightness and relaxed, easy interaction, and a husband must provide it.

THE HALAKHIC ELEMENTS OF
THE *MITZVA* OF *ONAH*

While each woman is unique, the halakhic literature identi-
fies a number of elements of intimacy that are generally pleasing to a woman.

Specifically, the following three ingredients are invaluable in creating the proper mood that the Torah desires:

1. רצוי דברים—LIGHT, EASY, LOVING
CONVERSATION (WORDS OF PRAISE, ETC.)

The Sages provide guidelines for this element of intimacy: the
conversation should please her and increase her desire for
intimacy (*Chagigah* 5b, *Brachot* 62a; Ran and Sheeta Mekubetzet to *Nedarim* 20a), and should increase his desire for her
(Rosh and Sheeta Mekubetzet to *Nedarim* 20a).[6]

> Rav chatted lightly and joked with his wife (Rashi: ap-
> peasing words) before having intimacy. (*Brachot* 62a)
>
> . . . One who is intimate with his wife needs to appease
> her and please her with words so that she not be unim-
> portant to him; and if he does not do this, then he
> should not be with her—all this in order that their wills
> should be as one without any mental coercion . . . It is
> not appropriate for a husband to approach his wife
> without pleasing, appeasing words. . . . (*Zohar, Bereshit*
> 49b)
>
> "And Adam said, 'This time . . .'" (*Bereshit* 2:23): These
> are pleasant words to make her agreeable and to bring
> her close to his will, to arouse love with her. See how
> pleasant those words are, how much they are words of

love, "bone of my bones and flesh of my flesh" to show her that they are one and there is nothing separating them. He then begins to praise her "She shall be called woman," she is the one of which none are alike, she is the honor of the home . . . These are all words of love, as it says "Many women did great things, and you arose above them all" (*Mishlei* 31:29), "A man shall therefore leave his father and mother and cleave with his wife," all of [these words are said] in order to draw her with love and cleave with her. (*Zohar, Bereshit* 49b)

It seems from the Zohar [see previous two entries] that according to the Torah it is imperative to speak to her with words of love so that in their desire they should be as one. The obligation is to delight her with words. (*Derech Pikudecha*, Positive *Mitzvah* #1)

You should first create an atmosphere, speaking to her in a manner which draws her heart after you, appeasing her, making her happy, thus binding her thoughts to yours. It is fitting to say some things that will arouse her and generate love and desire, and some things that will inspire her with awe of Heaven and pious, modest behavior. . . ." (Ramban)

Also *after intercourse* he should continue to chat lightly and lovingly with her in order that she not think that his whole intent in speaking this way earlier was for the sake of his own pleasure. Therefore, to counter this mistaken notion, he should continue to appease her even after intercourse. (*Damesek Eliezer*)

Significantly, the Sages' permission of conversation between husband and wife during intimacy does not allow discussion of any and all topics. The halakhah only permits conversation of an intimate nature; talk of other subjects during intimacy is strongly condemned by the Talmud (see *Chagigah* 5b). The Talmudic commentators explain the reason for this condemnation: talk of other subjects will distract them away from the intimacy they should both be fully focused on.

2. חיבוק ונישק—HUGGING AND KISSING

He must introduce every intimacy with hugging and kissing . . . in order to please his wife and arouse love between them. . . . (Yaakov Emden)

"החיבוק והנישוק או שאר עניני קורבה הם חלק וסעיף ממצות עונה, כמבואר ביורה דעה סימן קפ"ד."

. . . hugging and kissing and other aspects of intimacy are an integral part of the *mitzvah* of *Onah*, as explained in *Shulchan Aruch, Yoreh De'ah* 184 . . . (Y. Y. Kanievsky)

Closeness in the way of hugging and kissing also constitutes part of the obligation of *Onah*, and it is [part of] the *mitzvah* of pleasing his wife." (*Igrot Moshe, Even HaEzer* 4:66)

3. קירוב בשר—"PHYSICAL CLOSENESS" (THEY SHOULD BE TOGETHER, UNCLOTHED, UNDER ONE COVER)

R. Yosef taught: "*shearah*" (*Shmot* 21:10)—this refers to physical closeness: that is, he should not behave like the Persians who have intercourse while they are clothed. (*Ketubot* 48a)

Ritva: . . . even if he does this (remains clothed) out of a desire to be modest, for this is not the loving, affectionate way of being intimate.

Her physical intimacy ("*kiruv basar*"—the Sages say this is the meaning of "*shearah*"), the cover of herbed ("*k'sutah*"), and her time of love ("*onatah*") he may not withhold from her, for this is the "manner of daughters." (Ramban on *Shmot* 21:10)

If a man says, "I only desire to be intimate while I and she are clothed"—he must divorce her and give her the amount of money specified in the Ketubah. Note by Rema: Similarly, if she says, "I only desire to be intimate while I and he are clothed"—she is divorced and forfeits her Ketubah. (*Shulchan Aruch, Even HaEzer* 76:13)

They must both be naked during intimacy. Those who are intimate while clothed are behaving like the Persians. If a man says, "I only desire to be intimate while I and she are clothed" —he must divorce her and give her the amount of money specified in the Ketubah, because the Torah requires specifically that there be physical closeness. (R. Yaakov Emden)

We learn from the translation of "*shearah*" [given above] that [if one fails to provide this] it is as if he did not fulfill the *mitzvah* of *Onah* at all. (*Chelkat Mechokaik, Even HaEzer* 76:13)

They must, however, both be covered—together—under one sheet or covering.

Their physical intimacy must be covered. (*Zohar, Pinchas* 226a)

The Almighty is displeased with four [groups of people] . . . : one who is intimate unclothed *without a cover.* . . . (*Otzar HaMidrashim—Chupat Eliyahu Rabbah*, p. 164

and *VaYikra Rabbah* 21:8, quoted by Tosafot in *Niddah* 17a)

He must cover himself [their intimacy] with a sheet or cover of any kind even when it is night and when it is dark. In fact, even when he is alone, he must be covered in order to be modest. (R. Yaakov Emden)

THE PAIN OF REJECTION: A DEFINITION OF *ONAH*

R. Rechumi, who was learning at Rava's *yeshivah* in Mechoza, used to return home every Erev Yom Kippur. Once, he was so involved in his learning that he forgot to return home. His wife was expecting him, saying, "He is coming soon, he is coming soon." As he did not arrive she became so depressed that tears began to flow from her eyes. R. Rechumi was at that moment sitting on a roof. The roof collapsed under him and he was killed. (*Ketubot* 62b)

In the midst of its discussion of the *mitzvah* of *Onah*, the Talmud relates this incident and describes the punishment R. Rechumi received for the anguish he inadvertently caused his wife. Perhaps the Talmud, through its account of this incident, wants to inform us of the strict Heavenly punishment for one who neglects—even unintentionally— his responsibility to his wife.

But an obvious question presents itself: who suffered the most from R. Rechumi's severe Divinely executed punishment? If his temporary delay in returning pained her, then how much more so must this permanent absence have hurt her!? Where, then, was the Divine justice and compassion for R. Rechumi's wife that motivated the Heavenly intervention in the first place?

Perhaps we can suggest that the Talmud wishes to teach us another, deeper lesson as well—perhaps this episode provides us with the fundamental definition of what the *mitzvah* of *Onah* is and what it is designed to do.

Consider: before the news of R. Rechumi's fatal accident reached his wife, what feeling more than any other characterized her emotional state? She was hurt because she felt rejected. The sacrifices she made in order to enable her husband to learn were enormous; the time they spent together was very brief and fleeting and, therefore, infinitely more valuable and important to her and, no doubt, to her husband. As she waited, though, a horrible thought assailed her—perhaps her husband didn't value this short time together at all; perhaps he would rather remain in the Yeshivah than return home even for this short visit. The feeling of rejection welled up inside her and she began to cry.

Later, she received news of her husband's death. She mourned his death, to be sure. But deep, deep down in her heart, she was comforted, too, because now she was sure she knew the real reason why her husband had not returned home—he hadn't come back because he *couldn't* come back. Had he been alive, he certainly would have kept—happily, enthusiastically—their appointment; nothing short of death could have kept him away. She mourned him, but now the feeling of rejection was gone. The Almighty, in His compassion for her, removed that sense of rejection that had tortured her—*for nothing is as painful as rejection.* Rejection is painful to every person, but never more so than when a wife feels that her husband does not desire her.

This episode was related here, in the midst of a discussion of the *mitzvah* of *Onah*, in order to teach us what the essence of the *mitzvah* of *Onah* is. A husband fulfills the *mitzvah* of *Onah* by ensuring that his wife *never* feels rejected;

the *mitzvah* of *Onah* requires—*demands*—that a husband communicate to his wife that he loves, cherishes, and desires her passionately. The word "*Onah*" means, literally, "time." A husband fulfills the *mitzvah* of *Onah* when he sets aside and devotes a period of time in which he focuses solely on his wife—to the exclusion of everything else in the world.

There is only one natural, logical barometer that indicates the success or failure of a husband's observance of *Onah*: his wife's happiness, sense of security, satisfaction, fulfillment, and confidence.

The ambiance created by the Torah through its legislation of the *mitzvah* of *Onah* stands in stark contrast to the sexual milieu characteristic of the non-Jewish world.

In the selfish (sexually, and otherwise) world, each partner is busy grabbing everything he can get out of the relationship for himself in his single-minded quest to make himself "happy." A spouse is little more than a means to obtain self-gratification. Intimacy becomes a sexual tug-of-war, with the inevitable result that it awakens the feeling of being used and exploited, and not cared for at all.

Contrast this to the Torah's system. A husband is focused solely on satisfying his wife, investing marital intimacy with as much pleasure, love, loyalty, security, etc. as he can. And, while a woman is not subject to a *mitzvah* comparable to the *mitzvah* of *Onah*, human nature—and especially a woman's nature—is such that there is a natural desire to reciprocate and give pleasure to the one who is so intent on, and devoted to, providing you with attention, importance, and pleasure. In the Torah's scheme, then, each spouse is busy trying his or her best to give the other spouse the maximum of love and pleasure, with the result that both marriage partners are happy and united.

How different the two philosophies are! One system leads to short-term (albeit much publicized and glamourized) sexual gratification and long-term (unpublicized, but well-documented) mistrust, frustration, and dissatisfaction; the other leads to short- and long-term sexual gratification, trust, satisfaction, confidence, security, marital and psychological stability, peace of mind, and harmony.

What, ultimately, contributes to the striking success of the Torah's stable, secure marriage?

That which contributes to the creation of the incomparably successful Torah marriage is nothing other than the sexual drive and the way in which the Torah directs the raw, instinctual, untamed sexual drive into all of the desirable, sublime benefits and blessings we described.

Without the infusion of the *Yetzer Hara*'s enthusiasm and passion, marital intimacy is performed "merely to observe the *mitzvah* of *Onah*" (Rashi, see chapter 6) and does not have the capability to unite husband and wife. No amount of Torah alone can do the job, just as no amount of spice alone could satisfy without the food it is meant to accompany. Without the guidance and direction of the Torah, intimacy quickly degenerates into a selfish, indulgent and, ultimately, divisive act. Only in the synthesis of these two can we realize the manifold blessings that marital intimacy can bestow.

This is an incomparable accomplishment of the Torah's system. This is the intent behind the Almighty's declaration that "I created the *Yetzer Hara*, and I created the Torah as its spice." This is the fulfillment of the Almighty's command to serve Him with both *Yetzers*, the physical/instinctive and the intellectual/deliberate. This is authentic, uncompromised holiness.

8

──────────────────────

Guarding the Treasure

> There are eight things [which share the same charac-
> teristic] that an overabundance of any one is not good,
> whereas the proper, moderate amount is very good; and
> these are they: . . . (2) intimacy. . . . (*Gittin* 70a)

How do you guard a treasure? Use it sparingly, handle it
tenderly, take it out only on special occasions, keep it out of
general eyesight, hide it away in a private, secret place.

Intimacy is a precious gift from the Creator; it is a delicate treasure He graciously bestowed upon humanity. And,
as with all treasures, it must be carefully guarded to ensure
that it not lose its sheen or luster.

In addition to giving us a gift, the Almighty taught us
how to protect His gift. The enjoyment of intimacy and the
receipt of its manifold blessings are dependent upon many
delicately balanced factors, and the dangers that threaten to
disrupt this balance are legion. This chapter discusses briefly

some of the Torah's safeguards against the misuse and bru-
talization of intimacy.

NIDDAH

A woman becomes a *niddah* at the onset of menstrual bleeding, from which point sexual relations as well as all other forms
of physical contact between husband and wife are forbidden.
After all menstrual bleeding has stopped, a woman observes
seven consecutive clean (no menstrual bleeding) days. Until
such time as the bleeding completely ends, a woman cannot
begin her count. The *halakhah* prescribes a minimum of five
(four, in some Sephardic communities) days from the onset
of *niddah* before the counting of seven clean days can begin.
After these (minimum of) twelve days have elapsed, the
woman immerses in a kosher *mikvah* and leaves the *niddah*
state. Physical contact and intimacy are now permitted.
Counting seven clean days and proper immersion in a kosher
mikvah are indispensable prerequisites to leaving the *niddah*
state. Even after seven clean days have elapsed, failure to
immerse in a kosher *mikvah* prevents a woman from leaving
the *niddah* state.

Intercourse with a *niddah* carries with it a severe penalty—*kahret*—spiritual excision from the destiny of the
Jewish people.

Perhaps the greatest threat to the sexual relationship in
marriage is overindulgence and overfamiliarity. "Familiarity
breeds contempt" in all realms, and certainly no more so than
in matters sexual. And, today, when Western society seductively
and enthusiastically offers satisfaction of every sexual fantasy
and appetite outside of marriage, intimacy with one's spouse

soon seems dull and unexciting. The "seven-year itch" has become the "three and a half-year itch," with all the heartbreak that tragic statistic brings with it.

The institution of *niddah* protects a Jewish couple from the dangers caused by overindulgence.

In addition, the faithful observance of *niddah* brings with it many more happy benefits, some of which I described in my book, *Table for Two*.

The Sages, with their keen insight into human nature, enacted protective measures, called "*harchakot*," in order to ensure that husband and wife do not engage in certain activities that could, possibly, culminate in their being intimate in violation of the Torah's prohibition. The *harchakot* are quite specific and comprehensive in their scope. The observance of these *harchakot* is an absolute must mandated by halakhah. Sadly, some people observe the *harchakot* halfheartedly, or not at all. (See *Shulchan Aruch, Yoreh De'ah* 195 for a description of these *harchakot*.)

It is, perhaps, worth noting that no *harchakah* prohibits courtesy, gentle speech, or consideration during the *niddah* period. Relating to one's wife with "*mentschlichkeit*" during this period violates no halakhic prohibition; its absence, in contrast, violates dozens. In fact, the *niddah* period calls for heightened sensitivity and consideration, as the onset of *niddah* means the loss of an opportunity to conceive a child, a traumatic and discouraging disappointment for many women.

As we have noted many times, the proper behavior of husband and wife during the *niddah* period—their meticulous observance of the laws and spirit that characterize this time—assures that their intimacy, when they reunite, will be infinitely more enjoyable and meaningful. This is the fulfill-

ment of the Torah's promise that "she will be as beloved to
him as she was when she entered the *chupah*."

YICHUD

Many times throughout Torah literature, sexual desire is likened to fire. Fire is a powerful force. If it is used with great
care, caution, and intellect, fire can be a great force for good.
Unchecked, fire quickly reverts to a catastrophic force for
destruction.

Sexual desire operates in much the same way. Under the
guidance of the moral and intellectual faculties that adhere
to the Torah's directives concerning marital intimacy, sexual
desire can be used to attain great spiritual heights, accomplishment, and great happiness. Cut loose from that controlling
intellect, sexual desire can wreak unparalleled havoc.

There are situations in which desire can overwhelm the
tenuous control exercised over it by the rational, moral, and
intellectual faculties. No person is immune to the vertiginous
effect of sexual desire. As the Sages proclaim, *"Ein apitropus
l'arayot"* (No one can be a guardian against sexual unchastity).

> When the Sages said, "the greater the person, the more
> powerful his evil inclination," they were referring
> specifically to sexual desire . . . and one requires great
> strength [of will] and great safeguards in order to
> escape the many snares of its temptations in these
> matters. . . . (R. Moshe HaMakiri, *Seder HaYom*)

We don't serve our passions. A Jew—a human—thinks
with his or her brain, not with his or her hormones. We re-

ject any situation, atmosphere, or environment that is optimal for acting on the basis of impulsive sexual desire, unen-
cumbered by reasoned restraint.

The laws of *yichud* forbid any man and woman who are
not married to each other to be alone together in an isolated,
secluded place. Immediate blood relations are not included
in this prohibition; relatives by marriage are. Any man and
woman who are forbidden to consummate a physical relationship are subject to the prohibition of *yichud*.

FORBIDDEN RELATIONSHIPS

The Almighty, in *Parashat Acharei Mot* (*VaYikra* 18:6–18),
forbids marriage and sexual intimacy with certain members
of one's own extended family. Violation of these prohibitions
carries the severest penalties.

R. Shimshon Rofoel Hirsch, in his commentary on
Chumash (*VaYikra* 18:6), provides a rationale for the Torah's
prohibition of these forbidden relationships:

> Amongst the factors that raise into the sphere of holy
> and sanctifying Mitzvahs what otherwise would belong,
> as "ervah", to crude animal life, surely must be reck-
> oned as not the least, the fact that the bodily union of
> the sexes at once lays the foundation for the purest, most
> intimate, strongest spiritual union of the minds and
> hearts of two beings. It lays the foundation for that blos-
> soming which our marriage-blessing celebrates as "love,
> companionship, peace, and deep friendship", and which
> forms that sublime conjugal love which [is] "stronger
> than death and which all the stormy floods of fate can-
> not quench". In short, the "and he shall cling ("davak")

to his wife" loses all "ervah"-sensuality and becomes invested with the highest moral dedication, if it does really effect that wonder of wonders, that "and they shall be as one flesh" on which all true family happiness and national happiness builds itself up. Hence the less there is in existence before marriage any bond of attachment of family love, the more that the strongest form of attachment starts with marriage, the more does the sexual side of marriage become a basic factor in the whole moral sphere of happy married life full of love in every phase. It starts and is brought about by it and elevates it to the realm of pure morality.

But where there is already the affection of parents, brothers and sisters, and relatives, in the ordinary course of nature, attaching hearts and feelings to one another— and the purer and more truly the family life of the priestlike People of God exercises its moral influence, the stronger and farther reaching will the pull of this family love be—marriage will only have to bring some weak addition to this love. Love will have been there before, and marriage will add almost nothing more than the sexual element, which by itself alone without bringing about the miracle of the loving union of two beings, sinks down to naked "ervah".

And again, parental, brother and sister love, family love, altogether the mission and influence of parents, brothers and sisters, children and relatives, form, by themselves, apart from conjugal love and the conjugal mission, such important independent factors on the pure and mutual working and effect of the family life which God's Torah aims at producing, that it can not approve or tolerate the misplacing of any one of these factors. A mother can not become a wife without ceasing to be a mother, a sister can not be a wife without ceasing to be a sister, an aunt can not become a wife

without giving up being an aunt etc. etc. But mothers, sisters, aunts, etc. are to remain as such. But a sexual union with them which does not allow them to become wives would become nothing more than mere "ervah."
. . . (R. Hirsch, *The Pentateuch*, Leviticus pp. 485–486)

What does the sexual component of marriage add in these proposed relationships? Nothing, R. Hirsch explains, except sex. The emotional component—a loving feeling of attachment, the *devek* that intimacy is designed to create— already exists between this man and woman by virtue of the earlier familial relationship they share. Sexual intimacy, then, is an end in itself, and sex devoid of its emotional, *devek*-producing dimension does not enjoy the Torah's respect or permission. The parallel between R. Hirsch's explanation of the Torah's prohibition against the forbidden relationships and our discussion of the Torah's condemnation of the nine *middot* is clear.

PREMARITAL SEX

Premarital sex suffers from all of the deficiencies we have described in this book. Apart from the immediate concerns of violating strict Torah prohibitions (among them sexual intimacy with a *niddah*), the many long-term psychological and spiritual consequences are devastating. We will limit our discussion to a brief survey of some of those psychological consequences.

The Torah forbids sexual intimacy outside of marriage, and even non-Jewish Western society (once heir to a certain moral decency) condemned such liaisons as late as several decades ago (at which time, sadly, the last traces of whatever

biblical refinement Western society had once possessed were
finally completely and effectively obliterated). To engage in
premarital sexual activity is to cultivate an appetite, of enormous proportions, for the *ta'ama d'issura*, the taste of that
which is forbidden. And the enemy of sanctity, the near-
insurmountable obstacle to attaining sanctity, is an appetite
for the *ta'ama d'issura*. Premarital sex is exciting and attractive, in large part, because it is forbidden, morally and ethically. Marital intimacy, for one who possesses (or, rather, is
possessed by) an appetite for the experience of that which
is forbidden, is *neither* exciting *nor* attractive for exactly the
same reason—because it is *not* forbidden. Once the enjoyment
of sex becomes a function of the degree of its forbiddenness
(the legacy of the *ta'ama d'issura*), then marital intimacy cannot long fulfill or satisfy. This evil desire draws its victim from
one forbidden experience to another, ever seeking greater and
greater sources of "*issur*" (the forbidden) to satisfy its insatiable
hunger. What hope does marital intimacy have for such a
connoisseur of "*issur*"?

In addition, for the person who engages in premarital
sexual activity, there is no inextricable linkage between the
physical and emotional components of sexual intimacy. Premarital sex is sex without commitment. By definition, premarital sex is sex for its own sake. These pernicious seeds bear
equally odious, noisome fruit years later after marriage. The
definition of sanctity in sexual matters given by the Vilna
Gaon—"sanctity is avoiding the nine *middot*"—seems simple
enough. It is not. Sanctity requires that *every* intimacy must
create *devek*, must strengthen the emotional commitment and
solidify the marital bond between husband and wife. Main-
taining this single-minded emotional focus requires great

effort of will. To one trained in sex without commitment, to one steeped in sex for its own sake, it is nearly impossible.

One final consideration: The Torah condemns, as one of the nine *middot*, the union called "*b'nei arbuvia*" ("children of mixture," see chapter 6). "*B'nei arbuvia*" occurs when a husband thinks of another woman while having intimacy with his wife, and vice versa. For one who has had other sexual partners, it is infinitely harder to direct all of one's thoughts and attention exclusively to one's spouse; inevitably, comparisons are made. This intimacy between husband and wife is of the "nine-*middot*" variety, which, the Torah teaches us, cannot contribute to the strengthening of this marriage. The youthful practices of long ago come back to haunt, and threaten the integrity of, this marriage long after those practices have been abandoned.

One who steadfastly refuses to succumb to the tempting allure of engaging in premarital sex will be spared a lifetime of misery, angst, and turmoil.

> Who is wise? One who sees the long-term consequences of his actions. (*Tamid* 32a)

> The God of the Jewish people is an enemy of sexual licentiousness. (*Sanhedrin* 106a)

SEXUALLY EXPLICIT MOVIES, TELEVISION, THEATER, LITERATURE

Today, in our lowly spiritual state, there are people who read newspapers [etc. etc.] which contain pictures [and accounts of the behavior] of immodest, immoral women

[and men]; these pictures remain vividly, indelibly in
their minds, and the Evil Inclination conjures up those
obscene images in a person's thoughts during intimacy,
[contaminating and perverting the holiness of the inti-
macy] . . . It goes without saying how much more spiritually harmful it is to watch movies in which the immorality is actively, graphically depicted before one's
eyes. . . . (*Kli Milchama*)

Exposure to the brutal sexual excesses and perversion of
Western society through the various media distorts and adul-
terates (the word choice is exact) the purity and sanctity of one's
thoughts and attitudes toward sex. Constant incitement and
titillation desensitize. Preoccupation and imagination distract,
dilute, and enervate. A steady diet of ersatz gratification produces the ironic, pathetic state of being filled, but not fulfilled.

PHYSICAL CONTACT WITH A MEMBER
OF THE OPPOSITE SEX OTHER THAN
ONE'S SPOUSE ("*N'GIAH*")

The *halakhah* forbids physical contact of any form with a
member of the opposite sex other than one's spouse.
    Why? In what way does this prohibition protect the sanc-
tity of sex and the integrity of marriage? What harm, after all,
can a fleeting touch do? To forbid all such forms of social
interaction (superficial and, ultimately, meaningless interaction) seems inflexible, and cruel. Certainly, the insignificant
"thrill" contained in such a momentary encounter is unworthy
of the Torah's attention and legislation.

There are many reasons, similar to those mentioned in the preceding sections, for this prohibition. We will limit our remarks to one psychological observation.

Every stranger's incidental, casual, meaningless touch desensitizes one spouse to the *devek*-producing capability of a tactile encounter with the other, and robs the spouse's "mere" touch of its ability to catch and rivet one's attention. Often, people are so busy worrying about the loss of those myriad minor encounters that they forget to mourn the loss of something infinitely more precious: preserving the freshness and excitement of a spouse's sex appeal. The Torah hasn't forgotten.

In summary, the Torah's intent in prohibiting such activities as premarital sex, graphic movies, television, and *n'giah* is not to deprive or diminish the enjoyment of physical pleasure. Rather, the motivation behind these and other guidelines is to protect and enhance the sanctity, dignity, and enjoyment of marital intimacy. There are many activities and situations that ostensibly provide some form of sexual gratification while, in reality, they sow seeds of unhappiness and discontent and rob real legitimate sexual encounters of their ability to fulfill and satisfy. The cheap thrill is not cheap at all! Torah safeguards are designed to eliminate distractions that divert attention away from, and lessen the intensity and passion of, the one sexual relationship the Torah wants to maximize—that of husband and wife. The Torah knows what experiences will or will not provide the short-term and the long-term satisfaction, both physical and emotional, that people crave and seek (often without knowing what it is they seek so restlessly), and safeguards them. This keen insight by the Torah is not surprising, of course, since the Author of the Torah and the Creator of the human soul are One.

. . . Permitted intimacy provides real satisfaction—as opposed to forbidden intimacy which does not satisfy, and regarding such forbidden intimacy our Sages say, "there is a small organ in man: if it is denied, it is satisfied; if it is fed, it is hungry. . . ." (Kli Yakar, based on Rashi to *Bereshit* 39:6)

9

Pru Urvu

The reader may have wondered why "*pru urvu*" (procreation), another aspect of marital intimacy and itself a pivotal *mitzvah*, was not given more attention. In fact, this was done deliberately in order to emphasize the fact that the *mitzvah* of *Onah* is a *mitzvah* in its own right, quite apart from any considerations of procreation. This was done, not to minimize, God forbid, the importance of the *mitzvah* to have children, but, rather, to dramatize the importance of the *mitzvah* of *Onah*.

In reality, though, this entire book is about "*pru urvu*," because the conditions needed for the complete, successful observance of *Onah* are exactly those that are required for the complete, successful observance of *pru urvu*, for two reasons:

1. The thoughts of husband and wife during intimacy have untold profound, eternal influence, for good or, God forbid, bad, on the child that will result from that union. Indeed, the starting point for the Talmud's discussion of the nine *middot* is the premise that distracting, unworthy thoughts by either spouse at the time of conception will produce a child whose soul is spiritually blemished and that carries within it the lasting imprint of its parent's rebellious, disloyal thoughts. Although

it is always possible to transcend one's nature, it will be very difficult to do. What, then, should occupy the thoughts of husband and wife? Each spouse should focus on his or her tremendous, loyal, exclusive love and commitment to his or her spouse. This is true purity and sanctity in marital intimacy.

> One should know that according to the degree of holiness that he attains at the time of intimacy, to that degree will he impart a holy soul to his child [conceived from this union]. (*Reishit Chochmah*, *Shaar HaKedushah*, chap. 16)

> Our Sages have said that a man's thoughts and intentions during the time of conception will have their effect on the offspring: If he thinks impure thoughts, he will impart an unholy soul to the child born of that union; if his thoughts are pure, he will bring about the birth of a holy soul. (*Or HaChaim*, *Parashat Tazriah*)

> Because of their abundant love for each other during intimacy for the sake of Heaven, the child will be vigorous, clever, and beautiful. (Ramban)

> One should ease his wife's mind and make her happy, prepare her and nurture her with words that make her happy so that she feels passionate towards him (which will be apparent in her breathing and eyes). Then they will love each other, and their children will be wise: for their newborn child's cleverness or folly depends on their love for each other during intimacy. (R. Yaakov Emden)

> Only by increasing the desire [of one spouse for another] during intimacy [does one ensure that] the children will be righteous. (*Sefer Chassidim*, 362)

> "And Adam knew his wife again [עוֹד]; and she gave birth
> to a son, and called his name Sheit . . ." (*Bereshit* 4:25)

> Rashi cites a *Midrash* in *Bereshit Rabbah* (23:5): What does
> the [otherwise superfluous] word "עוֹד" (again, or more)
> refer to? It teaches you that God gave Adam increased
> desire for his wife.

Why did God increase Adam's desire for Chava? In light
of what we've just said, we can, perhaps, suggest an answer.
Kayin and Hevel, their first children, had not been worthy to
be the progenitors of the human race. No worthwhile strain
would come from them. Any hope for the continuation of the
human race must, therefore, lie elsewhere, in another, as yet
unborn, child. Therefore, in order to ensure that their next child
would be righteous and would, in fact, be a worthy successor
to Adam and Chava, the Almighty increased their desire for each
other, in accordance with the principle that "only by increasing the desire [of one spouse for another] during intimacy [does
one ensure that] the children will be righteous."

2. In addition, after birth, the correct observance of *Onah*
affects a child in another, equally important, way. The goal
of *Onah* is the production of *devek*, the unity of husband and
wife. A home filled with *devek* is characterized by tranquillity, stability, fidelity, contentment, and confidence. These are
the ideal conditions in which to nurture and shape a young,
impressionable character. A child's psychological, emotional,
and spiritual well-being are very much dependent on the
mood of his or her parents. A calm, tranquil home is far better equipped to produce happy, content children than a tur-
bulent home.

The *mitzvah* of *Onah* has profound consequences, then,

in both the "nature" and "nurture" aspects of a child's creation and development. Perhaps we can suggest that the two different explanations given by the *Ran* and the *Sheeta Mekubetzet* as to the identity of the "sinful, rebellious ones" referred to in the verse in *Yechezkel* ("And I will take out from among you those who rebel against Me and sin against Me" [*Yechezkel* 20:38], see chapter 6 above) parallel these two aspects of the child-rearing process. The *Ran* addresses the first aspect ("nature"), while the *Sheeta Mekubetzet* addresses the second ("nurture").

10

Conclusion

This book presents the rudiments of a Torah approach to marital intimacy, and is intended to serve as an introduction to the vast Torah literature on this complex, multifaceted subject with its inexhaustible wealth of information, instruction, insight, and inspiration. Our modest objective throughout has been twofold:

1. To introduce the fundamentals of Torah thought in this area and, in the process, dispel some popular, persistent misconceptions about the Torah's attitude to marital intimacy.

2. To stimulate further interest in, and study of, authentic Torah views regarding marital intimacy.

It is our fervent hope that this brief introduction will spark the reader's interest and curiosity and encourage him or her to pursue this subject further, from the original sources, under the direction of a competent Torah-true teacher.

Such discussion and instruction should become a standard feature of the classes that are given to young men and women before marriage. Of course, no class can substitute for the most desirable, discreet, personal means of instruction possible—transmission of the Torah's wisdom from parent to child, as the Almighty intended. It is our hope that here, too, this book can make some modest contribution.

> Just as one must be well-versed in the laws of *Niddah*, so, too, one must be fluent in the laws of *Onah* . . . (Zerach Eidelitz)

> Every person should be careful [in matters of intimacy], and he should caution his wife, sons and daughters, and all who listen to him . . . he should not be ashamed to speak about things concerning relations between husband and wife for the honor and sanctity of God . . . (*Pele Yo'etz*, on the letter *zayin*)

In the course of our discussion, we tried to understand some of the benefits that accrue from the meticulous observance of the Torah's laws governing sexual conduct between husband and wife. We must reiterate that observance of the Torah's laws must never be contingent upon our understanding or recognition of what benefits—material or spiritual—result from that observance. For the loyal Jew, it is enough to know that the Almighty commanded His people to obey these laws. No other motivation is needed.

This is not to say, of course, that God does not want us to invest intellectual effort in the study of His laws; on the contrary, such commitment to study the intricacies of the law as well as its philosophical bases and rationales served as the unconditional prerequisite for receipt of the Torah. Two times the Jewish people shouted "*Na'aseh*" ("We will scrupulously observe the *mitzvot*") (*Shmot* 19:8 and 24:3), to no avail. Only after they promised "*Na'aseh V'Nishma*" ("We will observe *and we will study them*") (*Shmot* 24:7), did the Almighty give His most precious possession to the Jewish people. We have engaged in the "*Nishma*," but a firm, uncompromising resolve and commitment to observe the Torah's *mitzvot* (the "*Na'aseh*") must always and unconditionally precede their study. Otherwise, we are not worshipping the Creator, but, rather, ourselves (see Rashi to *Shmot* 24:1 and Beit HaLevi on *Parashat Ki Tisa*).

Our Sages often refer to marital intimacy by the expression "*Derech Eretz*" (see, for example, *Eruvin* 100b, quoted in chapter 7). This expression is usually used in Torah literature to denote polite, refined behavior, that is, good manners. Why, then, do the Sages borrow this term and use it to describe marital intimacy?

"Good manners," *derech eretz*, requires that one transcend powerful innate emotions (jealousy, anger, impatience, and sadness, to name just a few) in order to display more pleasant, palatable, agreeable behavior out of consideration for the sensitivities of other people. Proper observance of the *mitzvah* of *Onah*, we have seen, requires a man to rein in some of the most powerful natural instincts and direct them in order to please and satisfy his wife. Sensitivity and attention to a woman's needs and desires determine when husband and wife will be intimate—not his libido or caprice. During intimacy, his *immediate* gratification gives way in the face of his responsibility to attend to her very specific needs. The ability to transcend and forgo the demands of the powerful sexual drive in favor of attending to the needs of one's spouse is, perhaps, the ultimate example of forgoing the satisfaction of one's own instincts out of consideration for the needs and sensitivities of others. This, as we said, is the very essence of good manners—*derech eretz*.

Psychological research indicates that approximately 70 percent of all troubled marriages suffer from some form of sexual dysfunction—either as cause or symptom of the break-down of the marriage. Even if marital intimacy problems are not the main reason for the disruption of *sholom bayit* (domestic tranquillity), nevertheless it is true that disruption can easily begin within the milieu of unpleasantness caused by intimacy problems. This is not to say, of course, that a healthy, pleasing, satisfying sexual relationship *alone* will produce or guarantee a healthy, pleasing, satisfying marital relationship. However, it is true that a successful marital relationship is quite impossible without the strength and support derived from a satisfying sexual relationship. Husband and wife interact on many different planes, and a happy, successful marriage means cooperation and harmony on each of those planes. A healthy sexual relationship is an essential, indispensable ingredient of the total marriage relationship.

The medieval Talmudic commentator Ra'ah (Ahron HaLevi) distinguishes between one who performs an activity without being aware of the fact that the activity is a *mitzvah*, and one who performs that selfsame activity aware of its *mitzvah* dimension. The second individual enjoys a certain spiritual protection that accompanies the performance of a *mitzvah*, while the first one does not.[1]

The same distinction applies to marital intimacy. Marital intimacy is a component of every marriage; all couples are intimate. But how they regard that intimacy makes all the difference. If they basically view it as a pleasurable pastime, then they remain unprotected from, and vulnerable to, all the dangers—philosophical and practical—the confused world presents. If a couple regard intimacy for what it really is (a *mitzvah*, service to the Creator, an integral part of a sanctified lifestyle), then this recognition and awareness brings with it its own protection against a myriad of dangers.

Marital intimacy is sacred. The Jewish people have guarded this fact for millennia. Open, frank, respectful discussion of marital intimacy in the Torah, Talmud, rabbinic literature, and the academies of Jewish learning inspired neither embarrassment nor shame, neither snickers nor sneers. Even in the face of various attempts throughout history to vilify and condemn sex as profane or sinful, the Jewish nation, through its steadfast observance of the laws of *Niddah* and *Onah*, has guarded, in principle and practice, the sanctity and dignity of marital intimacy.

The Talmud (*Brachot* 5b) relates a cryptic statement by the Tanna Abba Binyomin that "I was always careful to pray before my bed." This statement has been explained in a number of different ways in the commentaries. Perhaps his statement can also be explained in the following manner:

The Jewish outlook on life does not distinguish between the holy and the profane. Everything that exists has a spark of holiness, and can be used in the service of holiness. This righteous man did not "compartmentalize" his life into holy activities (e.g., prayer) and profane ones (e.g., bedroom activities, marital intimacy). Abba Binyomin did not assign marital intimacy to the realm of that which is unholy. His care to "always" pray "before his bed"—the latter a reference to his marital intimacy (see *Ketubot* 10b)—conveyed eloquently this unity. Contemplation of his bed inspired no shame. On the contrary, it, like his prayer, was holy. The two were not incompatible. Confronted by his bed, Abba Binyomin could, with head held high, pray with complete, clear-eyed confidence, in full knowledge that every moment of his life was lived "for the sake of Heaven." This is the uniquely Jewish view of marital intimacy (see *Sichot HaRan* 283).

R. Cahana was a disciple of the great sage Rav. The

Talmud (*Brachot* 62a) relates that R. Cahana once concealed himself under his Rebbe's bed in order to gain practical instruction and guidance in these most delicate and important matters. Rav discovered his zealous student when R. Cahana interjected a halakhic question regarding Rav's behavior. "Out, Cahana," Rav admonished, "it's not proper." Undaunted, R. Cahana replied, "This, too, is Torah and I need to learn."

The Talmud (*Kiddushin* 30b) compared the Torah to a *tavlin*, a spice, in relation to the *yetzer hara*, and, in chapter 4, we described the nature of this interrelationship. The analogy is exact in yet another way: even a small amount of spice can alter dramatically and enrich the taste of the food it accompanies. So, too, with Torah. Every additional amount of Torah knowledge and observance alters and enriches immeasurably the quality of one's life, refining and ennobling the instinctive, physical drives. (*Mesamchei Leiv*, pages 149–150).

As we mentioned, the Torah literature that discusses marital intimacy is vast. It is rich with instruction, both halakhic and ethical, in the Jewish way of marital intimacy. Each additional insight we glean is another opportunity to serve the Creator and enhance the quality of our lives, and we, like the talmudic sage R. Cahana, must proclaim, "This is Torah and I need to learn it."

תושלב"ע

Notes

CHAPTER 2

1. It should be noted that not all authorities in the Talmud agree to these interpretations regarding fasting and *nazir*. See *Ta'anit* 11a.

2. Why the Sages did not institute a *brachah* (blessing) before the performance of some *mitzvot* (among them giving *tzedakah* (charity), marital intimacy, etc.) is discussed by many rabbinic authorities. See, for example, *Mor U'Kitziyah* on *Shulchan Aruch Orach Chayim* by R. Yaakov Emden and *Derech Pikudecha*, Positive *Mitzvah* #1.

3. Avraham Avinu performed *Priah* although he had not been commanded to do so. During Moshe's generation it was practiced as a part of the Oral Torah. In Joshua's time, it was merely given the status of Written Torah, as no really new law could be introduced after the closing of the Torah. (See *Tosafot* on *Yevamot* 71b.) R. Hirsch's analysis is based on the progression of stages in the Written Torah.

4. We will examine "the instructions of our Sages" in chapters 6 and 7.

CHAPTER 3

1. Because now, clearly, his performance of *mitzvot* would be seen and understood for what it was (observance motivated by love of the Almighty), and could not be misconstrued as the mechanical discharge of an onerous burden.

2. In fact, the *halakhah* does not disqualify an unmarried Cohen from working in the Temple. Only a married Cohen Gadol (High Priest), however, may perform the Temple service on Yom Kippur.

3. But not enough to create a *ta'ama d'issura* because she will soon be permitted to him.

4. Holiness in the context of intimacy will be defined in chapter 6.

CHAPTER 4

1. Some clarification is in order here: Our concern in life is serving the Creator, and this analogy certainly does not mean to imply otherwise. The analogy is merely considering what ingredients are necessary in order to serve Him properly and fully.

2. This *yetzer* is often directed to evil, but it is not itself intrinsically evil.

CHAPTER 5

1. Yaakov Avinu had many children while he lived in Lavan's house.

CHAPTER 6

1. After seven clean days (free of bleeding) and immersion in a *Mikveh*.

2. R. Meir's answer does not imply exclusivity. For other insights in the realm of philosophical speculation, see, for example, *Sefer HaChinuch Mitzvot* 166 and 207, and Ramban's commentary on *Vayikra* 18:6, 19.

3. The *halakhah* prescribes a minimum waiting period of five days (in some Sephardic communities, four days), after which time, if all bleeding has stopped, the count of seven clean days can begin.

4. Jewish tradition teaches that Adam and Chava were originally created as one unified being, after which their different essences were separated out into two distinct beings. See Rashi to *Bereshit* 1:27.

5. Holiness in the context of intimacy will be defined later in this chapter.

6. According to R. Yaakov Emden, this daytime practice is only allowed for kings and royalty.

7. R. Yaakov Emden prescribes several specific foods "for the purpose of awakening sexual desire and increasing one's procreative power".

8. See chapter 7 for a discussion of the nature of this talk.

9. Which has a numerical value of 9.

CHAPTER 7

1. The Talmudic discussion of this *mitzvah* appears in Tractate *Ketubot* (chapter 5). The Rambam counts this *mitzvah* as prohibitive *mitzvah* #262 in his *Sefer HaMitzvot* (see also *Hilchot Ishut* 12:2). The *Sefer HaChinuch* discusses it in *mitzvah* #59. The *Tur* and *Shulchan Aruch* delineate the halakhic parameters of this *mitzvah* in *Orach Chaim* 240 and *Even HaEzer* 25 and 76.

2. The verb used throughout rabbinic literature to describe the husband's role in intimacy is "לשמח" ("to please"). (See, for example, *Pesachim* 72b, *Baba Batra* 10b, *Kallah* ch. 1, *Zohar Yitro* 93b, and *Kedoshim* 81b. See also *Bereshit* 26:8 and Rashi there.)

3. As opposed to situations where extenuating circumstances beyond his control prevent him from fulfilling this obligation.

4. The Chazon Ish described this desire of a woman when he wrote, "A woman's nature is to derive pleasure from the way her husband cherishes her." Consequently, he concluded, the husband's duty is clear: "And, therefore, it is incumbent upon him to show her love and closeness through an abundance of conversation and appeasement."

5. Intercourse without the appropriate preparation is a blow struck against a wife's feelings.

6. This light, easy, relaxed banter must *not* contain any type of crude or vulgar speech. The Talmud forbids "*Nivul Peh*" (obscenity) in any and all circumstances (*Shabbat* 33a, *Pesachim* 3a–b and *VaYikra Rabbah* 24:7).

> Although it is permissible for a man to chat with his wife in order to please her or to increase his desire for her

. . . nevertheless, do not, God forbid, sully your mouth
by talking obscene or foolish words; instead, only private, modest words . . . intelligently and tastefully chosen." (*Damesek Eliezer*)

CHAPTER 10

1. The Meshech Chochmah (cited in chapter 2) bases
his explanation of the episode in Gan Eden on this statement
of the Ra'ah.

Bibliography

SELECTED HEBREW SOURCES

Bible and Commentaries

Mikraot Gedolot. The text of the Hebrew Bible, with Aramaic Targum and various commentaries.
Rashi (Shlomo Yitzchaki, 1040–1105).
Ramban (Moshe ben Nachman—Nachmanides, 1194–1270).
Ba'al HaTurim (Yaakov ben Asher, c. 1275–c. 1340).
Rokeach (Elazar ben Yehudah, c. 1165–c. 1230).
Kli Yakar (Shlomo Ephraim Lunshitz, ?–1619).
Ohr HaChaim (Chaim ben Attar, 1696–1743).
HaEmek Davar (Naftali Tzvi Yehudah Berlin, 1817–1893).
Beit HaLevi (Yosef Dov Soloveitchik, 1820–1892).
Meshech Chochmah (Meir Simcha of D'vinsk—Ohr Somayach, 1843–1926).

Midrashim

Midrash Mechilta.
   Birkat HaNetziv (Naftali Tzvi Yehudah Berlin—Netziv)
Midrash Rabbah.
Midrash Tanchuma.
Pirkei D'Rebbi Eliezer.
   With *Midrash Tzava'at* R. Eliezer, and commentary of
   Damesek Eliezer on Tzava'at R. Eliezer HaGadol.

Talmud and Commentaries

Babylonian Talmud.
Jerusalem Talmud.
   Korban HaEidah (David Fraenkel, 1704–1762). In standard
   editions of the Jerusalem Talmud.
   Pnei Moshe (Moshe Margoliot, ?–1781). In standard editions
   of the Jerusalem Talmud.
Rishonim—Early Talmudic commentators, 10th to 15th cen-
   turies.
Rashi (see above). In all editions of the Talmud.
Tosafot. Analyses and commentary by French and German
   scholars of the 12th and 13th centuries. In all editions
   of the Talmud.
Rosh (Asher ben Yechiel, 1250–1327).
Ran (Nissim, c. 1290–c. 1375).
Ritva (Yom Tov ben Avraham, c. 1320).
Sheeta Mekubetzet (Betzalel Ashkenazi, c. 1520–1592).
Maharsha (Shmuel Edels, 1555–1631). In most editions of
   the Talmud.
Maharal (Yehudah Loew of Prague, c. 1526–1609).

Ein Yaakov (Yaakov ben Chaviv, c. 1445–1516). A compila-
tion of all the aggadic material found in the Talmud.
Iyun Yaakov (Yaakov Reisher, c. 1670–1733).
Be'urei Aggadot (Eliyahu ben Shlomo—the Vilna Gaon,
1720–1797).

Codes and Commentaries

Mishneh Torah of Rambam (Moshe ben Maimon—Maimo-
nides, 1135–1204).
Sefer HaChinuch (Attributed to Ahron HaLevi of Barcelona,
14th century).
Tur (R. Yaakov ben Asher, c. 1275–1340). This work has four
divisions: *Orach Chaim, Yoreh De'ah, Choshen Mishpat,
Even HaEzer.*
Beit Yosef (Yosef Karo, 1488–1575). In standard editions of
the Tur.
Shulchan Aruch (Yosef Karo, 1488–1575). An abridged version of the *Beit Yosef* commentary on the *Tur*, divided
into four divisions (See *Tur*, above).
  Rama (Moshe Isserles, c. 1520–1572). In standard editions
  of the *Shulchan Aruch.*
  Chelkat Mechokeik (Moshe Lima, 1605–1658). In standard
  editions of the *Shulchan Aruch.*
  Magen Avraham (Avraham Gombiner, 1637–1683). In stan-
  dard editions of the *Shulchan Aruch.*
  Mor Uketziah (Yaakov Emden, 1697–1776). In standard
  editions of the *Shulchan Aruch.*
  Biur HaGra (Eliyahu ben Shlomo—the Vilna Gaon,
  1720–1797). In standard editions of the *Shulchan
  Aruch.*

Chochmat Adam (Avraham Danzig, 1748–1820).
Mishnah Berurah (Yisrael Meir HaCohen Kagan—the Chafetz Chaim, 1838–1933). Commentary on the *Orach Chaim* section of the *Shulchan Aruch*.
Igrot Moshe (Moshe Feinstein, 1895–1986).

Ethical, Philosophical, Mystical Literature

Zohar.
Tikkunei Zohar.
   Commentary of Vilna Gaon
Moreh Nevuchim (Rambam).
Ba'alei HaNefesh (Avraham ben David—Ravad, c.1125–1198).
Sefer Chassidim (Yehudah HaChassid, ?–1217).
Iggeret HaKodesh (Attributed to Ramban).
Menorat HaMaor (Yitzchak Abuhav, 14th century).
Reishit Chochmah (Eliyahu de Vidas, 16th century).
Pele Yo'etz (Eliezer Papo, 17th century).
Siddur Beit Yaakov (Yaakov Emden, 1697–1776).
Even Shleimah (Eliyahu ben Shlomo—the Vilna Gaon, 1720–1797).
Sichot HaRan (Nachman of Breslov, 1772–1810).
Derech Pikudecha (Tzvi Elimelech Shapira, published in 1851).

Modern Sources

Hebrew

Aviner, Shlomo. *Etzem MeAtzmy*. Jerusalem, 1984.
Kanievsky, Yaakov Y. (the Steipler Gaon, 1899–1985). *Iggeret Kodesh Me'et Gedolei Yerushalayim*. Jerusalem, 1968.
Margaliyot, Y. A. Z. *Da'at Hakedushah L'haRamban*. Jerusalem, 1970.
Segal, Chaim Laib. *Mesamchei Leiv*. Jerusalem, 1992.

Shlenger, R. M. *Mishkan Yisrael*. Jerusalem, 1991.
Tzvi, C. B. *V'hiyitem Kedoshim*. Jerusalem, 1970.

English

Cowen, Alexander. *Tefillin*. New York: Merkos L'Inyonei Chinuch, 1967.
Friedman, Avraham Peretz. *Table for Two*. Jerusalem: Targum Press, 1992.
Goldberger, Moshe et al. *Techiyas HaMeisim*. Staten Island, NY: Yeshiva of Staten Island, 1990.
Goldwurm, Hersh, ed. *The Rishonim*. New York: Mesorah Publications, 1982.
Hirsch, S. R. *The Pentateuch*. Gateshead: Judaica Press, 1989.
Hirsch, S. R. *Collected Writings*, Vols. 1–5. New York: Feldheim Publishers,
Kaplan, Aryeh. *Waters of Eden*. New York: NCSY/Orthodox Union, 1976.
Lamm, Norman. *A Hedge of Roses*. New York: Feldheim Publishers, 1966.
Levi, Leo. *Torah and Science*. Jerusalem: Feldheim, 1983.
Miller, Avigdor. *Rejoice O Youth!* New York, 1962.
Shlenger, R. M. *Ohel Rachel*. Abridged version of *Mishkan Yisrael*, translated into English. 1994.
Steinsaltz, Adin. *The Essential Talmud*. New York: Basic Books, 1976.
Tendler, Moshe Dovid. *Pardes Rimonim*. New York: Judaica Press, 1979.
Weinbach, Mendel. "Teshuvah in Our Times" in *Living With Torah*, Vol. 2. Jerusalem: Jewish Student Information Center, 1993.
Wiesner, Naphtali. *In His Own Image*. New York: Mesorah Publications, 1992.

Index

ABOUT THE AUTHOR

Avraham Peretz Friedman received his semicha from the Rabbi Isaac Elchanan Theological Seminary of Yeshiva University and a master's degree in Electrical Engineering from Columbia University. He is the author of *Table for Two*. Rabbi Friedman studied and taught in Israeli Yeshivot for several years. He is currently the Rabbi at Duke University. He lives in North Carolina with his wife, Marsha, and their 4 children, Elisha, Adina, Ayelet, and Akiva.